MUSIC
—— for ——
WELLNESS

Feel the Music, See the Light

Suzanne B. Hanser

To my husband, Alan Teperow,
whose presence in my life and music in his soul
have sustained my wellness.

Berklee Press

Editor in Chief: Jonathan Feist

Senior Vice President of Pre-College, Online, and Professional Programs/
CEO and Cofounder of Berklee Online: Debbie Cavalier

Sound Engineer: Ayla Rose

ISBN: 978-0-87639-229-4

Berklee
Press

1140 Boylston Street
Boston, MA 02215-3693 USA
(617) 747-2146

Visit Berklee Press Online at
www.berkleepress.com

Berklee Online

Study music online at
online.berklee.edu

DISTRIBUTED BY

HAL•LEONARD®

Visit Hal Leonard Online at
www.halleonard.com

Berklee Press, a publishing activity of Berklee College of Music, is a not-for-profit educational publisher.
Available proceeds from the sales of our products are contributed to the scholarship funds of the college.

CONTENTS

ACKNOWLEDGMENTS

It has been a great privilege to live a life infused with music. My parents, Judy and David Blottner, introduced me to its magic when a piano appeared in our home, after surgery left me bedridden. As I explored the instrument as a way to heal, my teachers guided me not only in how to play music, but also how to feel the music.

In my determination to engage with music actively and interactively, I became a music therapist. I learned about this remarkable profession from masters of the art and science of music therapy, notably Donald Michel, Cliff Madsen, and Doug Greer. My students at Berklee College of Music and Berklee Online continue to be my dynamic teachers, whose life stories and creativity help me see the light through their words and musical compositions. I am most grateful to include a sampling in this book.

My colleagues and friends are sound advisors and guides. Those who were particularly instrumental in supporting me include: Sally Blazar, Suzy Conway, Amy Furman, Maria Hernandez, Robin Jacobs, Sheila Katz, Rebecca Perricone, and Elana Rosenbaum.

I am profoundly thankful to Ayla Rose, who worked at my side to engineer the audio excerpts that make the contributors' voices and instruments come alive. Suzi Mandel was an editorial companion who was generous in her feedback and discerning in her reviews. How wonderful to have her with me on this book! This project was only possible with the support of Debbie Cavalier and editorial prowess of Jonathan Feist at Berklee Press, as well as the staff at Hal Leonard who helped realize my vision of a book to read and hear.

The love of my family brings out my best. Thank you, Leora, Graeme, Jack, David, Eli, Shira, OB, Judah, Gabe, Jessie, Nava, Raviva, Evan, Noa, Tova, Alex, and Avi. The spirit of my son of blessed memory, Sam, inspires me always. My husband, Alan, feeds my mind, body, and spirit every day. I cherish you all.

PREFACE

Greetings, readers and listeners! I imagine that you picked up this book because you love music and have an inkling that it can enhance your wellness. You are probably aware that when you really feel the music, your mood can change in an instant. Perhaps your feet dance away or your mind swims with memories when you engage with music that is special to you. What is remarkable about music is that it can both energize and relax, excite and soothe, crystallize emotions that are hard to name and bathe you in memories. You can begin to see the light when you find a piece of music that tells you just how you feel. *Music for Wellness: Feel the Music, See the Light* is written for you lovers of music who wish to make music more a part of your life and make your life more whole through different musical experiences.

I make no assumptions about your musical background. It makes no difference whether you are an amateur, professional musician, or avid listener. Maybe you just love music and wonder why. To answer that question, this book offers you not just the opportunity to read relevant content, but to listen to music created by people like you and hear their personal stories about the creative process, inspiration, and how music contributes to their wellness.

Each chapter begins with a musical intention—a short piece of music to set the stage and the mood for the upcoming material. Within the chapters, you will be introduced to the people who composed the music and hear their stories. All of the music is original, and many of the examples are from individuals who are not musically trained and have recorded their music on iPhones or other handy devices. Most of them have been students in my online classes that enroll people from around the world or are training to become music therapists. So they cover a large spectrum across age, culture, and musical background. The stories about individuals who have been the beneficiaries of music therapy are true, but their names have been changed to preserve their privacy.

You can listen to the music and stories while you read, beforehand, and/or afterwards. You can read excerpts of the composers' stories while listening, or concentrate on each individually. These stories are excerpted, edited, or summarized for readability. To access the complete, raw, unedited narratives, in the contributors' own voices, please refer to the included audio files.

As you hear this original music, I hope you will be inspired to create your own, as the chapters suggest, and you will forgive the variability in quality of the music or recordings. This is music of people who are not necessarily performers, but creative souls who seek to develop and grow with their compositions, and have reflected on the impact of music in their lives. You will hear their stories in their own voices, and find out how they apply this music to enhance their own wellness.

Here is an introduction to the contributors, individuals of many ages and stages of life:

Pratham Aggarwal (he/him) has been immersed in music since the age of six, starting with singing and later exploring songwriting at thirteen. His compositions often delve into the challenges of high school and personal relationships, offering support and solace to his audience. As an incoming college freshman studying mechanical engineering, Pratham is passionate about creating music that soothes both himself and those around him, despite the demanding academic load. Drawing on his experiences growing up and living in New Delhi, India, Pratham aims to continue using his musical talents to connect with and uplift others throughout his engineering journey.

Nathan Chowilawu-Eshe (he/him) has been a lifelong student of music. With an experimental musical approach, Nathan uses cinematic sound, melodies, and harmonies to support focus, balance, comfort, and inner peace. In the moment-to-moment daily trek through life, Nathan believes music is the perfect partner for our wellness journeys. Creating music to support himself and others on their journeys is an honor and a pleasure. Nathan releases his wellness music with the pseudonym Chowla Blue. You can find music by Chowla Blue on major streaming platforms.

Gen Cleary (she/her) has spent more than twenty-five years in the entertainment industry as a lead creative mind, producer, and director. As a pioneer who helped the nightlife industry become a 1.3B$ success story on the U.S. West Coast, she was named in the top 16 most influential women in Las Vegas. She has worked closely with superstars such as Calvin Harris, David Guetta, Tiesto, Avicii, Martin Garrix, Kaskade, and Paul Oakenfold, and with brands, such as Disney, the Olympics, and Cirque du Soleil. Her company, Sound Connective, has a mission: To revolutionize the way we connect with sound through entertainment concepts.

Natalia de Rezendes (she/her) is an interfaith minister, music/voice teacher and vóvó (grandmother) of an absolutely "awesometistic" grandson named Nicky Mario. Having hailed from creatively loving Portuguese/Brazilian parents and so joyfully connected to her ethnic roots, she has spent most of her septuagenarian life helping to unveil the most powerful universal language on the planet—music—through song in the multitudinous languages of our beautiful world.

Marisabelle Díaz-Falcón (she/her) has always been moved by the emotional impact music can have on people. She started discovering this at a young age when taking violin lessons. Growing up in Puerto Rico, an island with music that is influenced by its mix of Spanish, African, and Taíno races, she has felt that her racial and cultural background has certainly shaped how she utilizes music as a clinical tool to promote a person's wellbeing through music therapy. Marisabelle hopes to continue shedding light on the impact of culture and race on health.

Frances Fiorino (she/her) leads activities for seniors with memory loss, realizing a long-held but unfulfilled dream of using music in her work. She previously enjoyed a career in aviation journalism and is a licensed private pilot. Music played constantly in her home. As a toddler, she would pull up on the bannisters of the stand-up radio, and put her ear up to the speakers. Her Italian father played opera; her mother, American Songbook songs and artists. She wasn't able to have piano lessons as a child, but pursued private piano/music studies through the years. Her passion is to broaden her knowledge and help others through music.

Mark Fuller (he/him) has served as a board-certified music therapist at Boston Children's Hospital since 2018, engaging in clinical care, program development and coordination, supervision of students and professionals, and clinical research. Mark received his bachelor's degree from Berklee College of Music and his master's in public health from Boston University. Mark is invested in improving the health and wellbeing of children and their families, and primarily provides music therapy to patients admitted to the cardiology service at Boston Children's. His research interests are in stress and coping in families of children with rare diseases.

Minxue Gao (she/her) began her musical journey at three years old, captivated by the enchanting sound of the piano. Immersed in classical piano for over fifteen years, she developed a deep connection with the instrument. As a music therapist, Minxue witnessed how music touched and transformed people of all backgrounds, soothing anxieties, providing solace, and fostering emotional expression. These revelations altered her life, shaping her career and perspective on the immense healing, empowering, and connecting potential of music. Committed to creating positive change, Minxue continues to walk her path as a music therapist, using her skills and passion to make a difference.

Samuel Gracida (he/him) is a music therapist currently based in Germany. He is originally from Mexico, and he spent a formative part of his life in China and the United States. Through many experiences around the world, as a musician and as a music therapist, he has seen firsthand the impact of music on people's lives. This has inspired him to work with businesses and organizations globally to promote harmony and healing to all those who need it.

Maria Hernandez (she/her) was born in Miami and raised in the Dominican Republic where her love for music and medicine was nurtured. After earning her medical degree, she pursued her music therapy studies to became a board-certified music therapist. She is currently developing a music therapy program at Mount Sinai Comprehensive Cancer Center, where she strives to interweave both her Cuban and Dominican cultures into her musical, medical, and music therapy experiences to enhance quality of life.

Mi-Lan Hoang (she/her) is studying to be a music therapist, as she fell in love with the idea of music as a means of improving health and wellbeing. Her biggest inspiration is her mother, whose work in both immigration law and occupational therapy taught Mi-Lan the importance of interdisciplinary solutions and collaboration between fields. Mi-Lan has a special interest in neuroscience and hopes to further develop musical techniques for rehabilitation and intervention. In conjunction with her passion for activism and social justice, her work centers around advocating for transdisciplinary research and therapy with art at the foundation of holistic care.

Shawn Kellner (he/him) is an Army Veteran with a twenty-five-plus year career in all facets of the music business. In 2019, he suffered a spinal cord injury that left his right arm paralyzed. Music has played a huge role in his recovery as he has had to relearn how to do everyday activities most people take for granted. In 2024, he will release an album called *World War Me*. This collection is a first person testimony about how "the stairway to heaven doesn't mean anything; it's the road back from hell that leads a man from death back to life." Music is the vehicle.

Marjorie (she/her) is fifty-seven, has been a stay-at-home mom for the past twenty-seven years to two wonderful and now grown children, and is excited to begin her second act. She is not a trained musician, but has loved music her whole life, inspired by her parents. In college, she majored in psychology and would love to combine that with her love of music to help others. Marjorie is now studying music therapy to try to learn how to use the healing powers of music to better people's lives.

Caitlin September Nugent (she/her) is a music teacher and aspiring music therapist. Her parents exposed her to a wide range of musical genres, and her father inspired her affection for poetry. While using music to help others grow has been a particularly rewarding and joy-filled part of her journey, Caitlin has discovered a passion for songwriting. She is the proud mother of a vivacious three-year-old boy, who has benefitted from music as a means of expressing himself. Caitlin looks forward to infinite years of mentoring and helping others, continued study, and creating powerful music that connects souls from all walks of life.

Nomuki Otganbayar (she/her) is an artist and songwriter from Mongolia. Her music career started at the age of nineteen, when she started to write songs. Her music inspiration came from many indie bands, and she wanted to connect her music with famous novels. When literature became a part of her soul, her imagination went wild and she decided to create a storytelling project and book of poetry, called *Eyelid*. She recently recorded an album of folk music, called *Evelyn*, that focuses on mental health and the relationship between our feelings and souls.

Tania Paz (she/her) is a singer-songwriter from Spain. She considers herself a musical nomad, as she has traveled the world to share her music with others. While living in South, Central, and North America, as well as several European countries, she integrated new styles and cultures into her expressive songs. Music is her life and her reason for being, and she expresses her most intimate and worldly wisdom through the universal language of sound and music.

Emily Sclar (she/they) is a queer, Jewish artist from Freeport, Maine, currently studying music therapy and performance at Berklee. Emily is a violinist and multi-instrumentalist who uses music as a way to express the complex feelings of being alive, through the art of songwriting and composition. They would describe themself as a sensitive being and empath, which has led them to use music as a way of healing and helping others. Emily is deeply passionate about this work and is excited to continue this journey of learning, creating, and expressing.

Tom Sweitzer (he/him) is the co-founder of A Place to Be, America's largest non-profit music therapy center. *Music Got Me Here* is a documentary about his work as a music therapist with a young man who had a traumatic brain injury. His one-person, off-Broadway show, *20 Seconds*, uses his true story of how music saved his life to teach people the real secret and magic behind music therapy. Tom enjoys writing children's musicals and is a true believer that performance itself is a tangible way for a person to feel heard and seen.

Hélène Vogelsinger (she/her) is a French electronic music producer and composer. After ten years of varied musical experiences, she trained in film music orchestration and video game sound design. She uses the modular synthesizer, an instrument that allows her to have an electronic orchestra at her fingertips and also to compose. She is a sound explorer, and her music is intense, spiritual, and hypnotic. It immerses listeners in an ocean of sounds that can lead to an altered state of consciousness. Her work links the past and the present, the memory of abandoned places, and the energy they release.

Zen Waqavonovono (he/him) is a Fijian-born musician who is deeply inspired by his roots as an indigenous Pacific Islander and by art as a form of free expression. He seeks to find new ways to weave his music, culture, and art to add to the growing voice of artists from the Pacific diaspora. Currently studying music therapy at Berklee College of Music, he hopes to one day take his clinical experience back home to contribute to the wellbeing of the people of Fiji.

June Westfield (she/her) is a storyteller and fantasy composer who uses ethereal textures and melodies to paint scenes of myth and magic. She draws inspiration from the woodlands and meadows of her current home in Michigan, as well as from her strong visual inner worlds and dreams. She is a visual artist as well as a musician, painting her own album art, and finds she expresses herself best with a combination of enchanting art and music.

Bea Wilderman (she/her) was born and raised on the Upper West Side of Manhattan in New York City. Her parents are from Sri Lanka, and she grew up with Sri Lankan drumming in the house. Her instruments include piano, guitar, drums, and voice. Bea has a B.A. from Yale University, an M.B.A. from Stanford Graduate School of Business, and a certificate in vocal technique from Berklee College of Music. Bea converted to Judaism as an adult, and has been an active member of the Jewish community both locally and nationally. Bea lives in Brookline, MA with her husband and two sons.

Bella Antonia Ybarra (she/they) is studying to be a music therapist, as they feel there is no greater healing power than music. Her heritage inspires her to share stories through music, and her family has always encouraged her to pursue her passion. They continue to help Bella realize her role in music and the role music has in her life. Bella also has an interest in cognitive psychology and vocal pedagogy, which they hope to utilize in their post-graduate education and in their clinical career. Bella hopes to share her passion for music with all who will listen.

I hope that you will find yourself in some of their narratives and connect to their revelations of how impactful music can be.

FOREWORD

By Dr. Lisa Wong

When I am tired, stressed, anxious, or simply seeking a moment of quietude, I go to music.

When I am seeking the answer to a question that seems just out of my reach, I go to music.

When I am trying to make sense of my world, I go to music. It may not be the same music each time, but differing in tempo, contour, harmony, or instrumentation. There may be lyrics to the music—or not. Perhaps it is the same for you. So many of us embrace music as a healing life force.

This is a book that invites us all to explore our relationship with music and deepen our exploration with—and love of—music.

When I first met Suzanne Hanser nearly twenty years ago, we worked with colleagues in the music and medical field to bring the voices of music therapy, music medicine, and music psychology together in one room, to share knowledge and ask questions together. I was struck by Suzanne's humility, her knowledge of music in the healing world, and her wisdom. Since then, we have traveled the world together and heard the same chorus everywhere: that music can touch lives in ways that words cannot.

Suzanne Hanser is one of the true pioneers of music therapy. As the founder of Berklee College of Music's highly respected Music Therapy department, the past president of the American Music Therapy Association, and now president of the International Association for Music and Medicine, she has shaped the trajectory and philosophy of music therapy around the world.

I can think of no better guide into this healing world than Suzanne.

This is more than a book. It is a journey, which gives agency to the reader/listener to navigate. Suzanne has curated a "choose your own musical healing adventure," that brings a remarkable set of music lovers and music therapists to journey with us. Depending on your mood, interest, and the time you want to invest, you can come back to this book over and over again, reading their stories, hearing their narratives, and listening to their music. As Suzanne so wonderfully puts it, you are invited to "Feel the Music and See the Light," all on your own time. Enjoy!

Lisa M. Wong, MD
Associate Co-Director
Arts and Humanities Initiative
Harvard Medical School

THE FUNDAMENTALS OF MUSIC FOR WELLNESS

Music was the first sound I remember. As an infant, I cried out for sustenance or cooed for a comforting touch, and my mother sang to me. She had a lilting soprano that she used almost constantly to communicate with me. Of course, I don't really remember any of this, but my mother told me of my first days when her dream of becoming a mother came true, and she sang in glorious thanks for a cuddly offspring to feed, soothe, and teach. She said my voice was musical, and I believe her, because music has been my companion throughout my life, accompanying me in my every mood, every day.

While not everyone considers music to be a language, I found that music communicated my needs and emotions with an authenticity that words could never match. You see, words are limited to the vocabulary that I have learned to speak, but music is a never-ending variety of sounds and patterns. While my words must be crafted analytically in grammatical phrases to be understood, I can express so many sensations through music that I could never find a word for. When I was ill as a child, my piano allowed me to voice my pain and isolation, as I improvised slow dirges in the low bass register. When I was frustrated, I would play fast trills in both hands up and down the keyboard, emulating the tremors of my anxious body. Music said what I didn't know how to say and what I didn't know I was feeling.

These primal connections with the piano fueled my ambition to make music with others and for others, leading me to a career as a music therapist. Training in music therapy gave me opportunities to meet people of many ages, life stages, conditions, ethnicities, and identities. By assessing their needs and designing treatment plans to meet clinical goals and objectives, I learned more every day about how impactful music could be in helping people live better and fuller lives. I was also witnessing some remarkable improvements in wellbeing, regardless of the physical or mental condition of the person with whom I worked. Music delivered a nonverbal and intuitive way of communicating beyond cognitive processing, and it forged a strong connection between us. Music was not just the bonding adhesive; it also provided a safe container for experimentation, as we explored the creative process and reflected on the meaning of the music. We could play in the liminal space—that transitional place between present and future, known and unknown—as the musical notes moved along and we reflected on what was happening in the mind, body, and spirit.

As a music therapist, I have had the honor of supporting many people who are unwell or living with serious life challenges, and I have witnessed the remarkable ability of music to accompany their journeys to wellness.[1] There are no cures or miracles to report, just the splendor of finding our creative selves and the inner music that gives us energy and life. Many of the strategies and techniques applied in music therapy are useful to all of us who cope with everyday stress, strain, and pain associated with living a full life. Music celebrates who we are and expresses what we want to hear. The lessons gathered from active music-making and composing, as well as reflective listening, can show us that when we feel the music, we see the light. This book presents some of those insights that music can teach us when we really listen and let it surround us with its beauty and awe.

I have never encountered anyone who didn't appreciate some form of music. They may not report that they have a particular connection to it, but they all respond to music in their own unique ways. Many claim that music transformed the way they approached life. You are probably reading and listening to this book because you believe that music has a role to play in enhancing your wellness, and you may have reached for an instrument or a playlist when you wanted to accelerate your biological tempo or feel more upbeat. That is just the beginning. There are many ways to apply music for wellness and we will explore a variety of approaches in this book.

To consider the influence of music on emotion, think of a movie without its musical score. I think you would agree that you are likely to be robbed of the suspense, romance, or other emotional context, when you are simply watching characters move about the set. Without a word, the score of a film sets you up for the entrance or exit of a character or an upcoming surprise. The effect can be immensely powerful, especially when an ominous melody or jarring rhythm scares us, or a sweet, flowing tune accompanies the blossoming of love. So consider your soundtrack—the music that you sang as a child or heard as a teen; music at that memorable concert, dance, or religious service; music that got you through all that traffic on the road; or music that eased you through high school. As you remember these times, I'll bet that you felt a change in your breathing or your heart rate. Maybe a smile came to your face. Throughout this book, you will be asked to reflect on your musical experiences and learn about yourself through your musical choices and challenges. Then, you can get creative yourself, with guidelines for how to apply music to influence your mood or manage your emotions.

When we tune into our inner talents and abilities, we can explore, express, and experiment with meaning through music. After all, music is a part of all of us. Our hearts beat in a tempo that sustains life by pumping our blood in a regular and predictable rhythm. In fact, a fast or slow heart rate or irregular pattern signals disorder, and must be attended to, in order to avoid blood clots, stroke, or chronic cardiovascular disease. Our body's metronome keeps our bodies working and in motion. If we develop Parkinson's disease or have a stroke, we may not ambulate with strict timing, and our gait can lose its methodical cadence and flow. An entire body of music therapy literature is actually devoted to Neurologic Music Therapy,[2] which utilizes techniques like "Rhythmic Auditory Stimulation"[3] to initiate a "go" response for the purpose of regulating the gait and promoting more efficient ambulation (more on this in chapter 3). This is only one of many music therapy strategies for wellness.

It is clear that music can affect us deeply, but do we intentionally apply music to help us get through a busy day, change our moods, or cope with distress? I tend to think that music is taken for granted. It follows us around in grocery stores, enticing us to stay longer and buy more, and in elevators, offering us relief from an uncomfortable silence amongst strangers. But when music is an intentional source of soothing, excitement, or anything in between, it can transform the way we approach life.

There are many ways to feel the impact of music on us, and shine a light on what we can learn about ourselves. Each of the chapters in this book investigates a particular function of music in our lives and provides strategies for experiencing these processes.

Music integrates body, mind, and spirit to discover our relationship to music and how it can enhance our lives and potentially change the world.

Before we explore these themes in greater depth and immerse ourselves in music-based interventions for wellness, it may be useful to understand how wellness is defined in the context of this book. The second part of this introduction lists some of the key terms I use to describe what this book hopes to achieve. The last section describes the interactive nature of the book and how to read and listen to its stories and samples of original music.

A PRIMER ON WELLNESS

The following definitions are provided here to elucidate processes associated with wellness from a psychological and scientific point of view. This section is atypical of the book's format, as it describes concepts without personal narratives and accompanying audio files. If you are interested in the thinking behind wellness, read on. If you are so inclined, you can skip this section and go directly to part I, where the stories of music and wellness begin. If you're game, I hope that you will find this scientific approach to wellness as fascinating as I do.

Wellness

To begin the lexicon, let's start with the term "wellness," directly from this book's title. The dictionary definition of "well" refers to a state of good health as a goal. As an adverb, it means in a good manner; as an adjective, pleasing or satisfactory; as an interjection, well, that's it!

I prefer to see the noun "well" like the cistern that gathers thirst-quenching water—that deep container where the end is often elusive and the flow of liquid appears endless. In the same way, I see wellness as an intentional quest to satisfy a thirst for an integrated body, mind, and spirit—a profoundly deep and intensive self-examination of the conditions that serve or do not serve this sense of wholeness, and the flow of self-compassion that is required in affirming life. In concert with the National Wellness Institute in the U.S.,[4] I acknowledge multiple dimensions of wellness:

- Physical
- Intellectual
- Emotional

- Social
- Occupational
- Spiritual

I have observed how it is possible to be well, even if your body is failing, or you are under tremendously stressful conditions. In my view, wellness is the wellspring—the font—of a full, lived life. It involves bringing conscious awareness and mindful attention to every moment and every move to the degree that it is possible. Wellness is not an outcome, but rather a practice, an opportunity to explore our understanding of the conditions that reside around and inside us. This requires us to take in how we are feeling, what we are thinking, and which perceptions arise, as we conceive of our world in a holistic manner.

Wellness offers us a chance to see us as we are and to be okay with that. When we look at ourselves in each moment, we have an opportunity to explore our humanity and our potential. It is this reflective muscle that I encourage you to exercise, as you are introduced to music strategies for wellness.

Whenever someone asks me how I am, I tend to answer quickly with an automatic "fine" or "okay." But I find myself wondering how I really am today and in this moment. I begin to check in. How is my body feeling right now? I stretch a little to see if there are any kinks in those bones or tension in the muscles. I bring my attention to my breath to gauge my tempo and rhythm. How long has it been since I took a long, luxurious breath? I start to observe the thoughts that have been swimming around in my head. Am I focused on the present or worrying about that upcoming deadline? What is this doing to or for my sense of wellness?

Stress

My practice to assess my wellness brings up the stress I am experiencing about meeting that deadline. I count up the consequences of not meeting that deadline. Focusing on the stress without creating a plan or starting the required work is making me feel what I call stress. Certainly, we cannot discuss wellness without addressing stress, a word that is so prominent in contemporary parlance that casual conversations often become competitions to see who has more stress: "I hold two jobs, and I never get any sleep" vs. "I take care of my mother and my children, I don't have any time for myself" vs. "I have so many deadlines that it is impossible to meet them and I'm going crazy." These statements reflect how universal stress is, and it can certainly be a threat to wellness. It is so pervasive that the National Institute of Mental Health (NIMH) has developed an "I Am So Stressed Out! Fact Sheet."[5] It reveals that stress is a natural response to threatening conditions, and anxiety is the body's reaction to stress, even when the stressor is no longer physically present. The fact sheet states that coping effectively with stress and anxiety is important to regulate and manage our emotions, as chronic stress can actually cause or exacerbate physical and mental illness.

It is no wonder that we use a word derived from engineering and physics to describe the strain that we go through in everyday life. From a physical perspective, stress is the amount of force placed on a unit, and that unit of material can be resilient or break apart. You can see how it describes the human condition, but as a psychological term, it has become ambiguous, as every stress response is unique. Stress carries strong negative connotations, but it is a necessary part of our adaptation to our environment.

I personally relate to a definition of stress by Kelly McGonigal in her book, *The Upside of Stress*. She explores how stress is what arises when something we care about is at stake.[6] For me, this perspective makes me feel that there is justification for the stress that can shake me up so badly. McGonigal points out that there are advantages to understanding and making friends with stress. When you see your response to stress as a "challenge response," you can realize how the heightened sensations, focused attention, and enhanced motivation that accompany stress can mobilize your energy. It does for me, anyway. McGonigal emphasizes how we can use stress to grow and learn, and how we can apply the social cognition and connections that arise from dealing with stress to change how we feel. It's all about making choices, once we turn our perception of stress upside down and see how it can serve us.

The Physiology of Stress

To better understand stress and what we can do with it, it is helpful to know something about the autonomic nervous system (ANS). As our bodies and brains adapt to the environmental stressors, the ANS automatically takes care of us. This complex network of involuntary activity happens without our lifting a finger or taking any conscious action. Two complementary segments do the trick: the sympathetic (SNS) and parasympathetic (PNS) nervous systems.

Famous for the fight-flight-freeze response, the SNS reacts to threats to our survival by activating those mechanisms that would physically prepare us to fight a wild animal, run away, or freeze in place. It signals us to breathe more rapidly. It pumps oxygen through our bloodstreams, accelerates our blood pressure, rushes blood supply to our muscles, and sends specialized hormones and chemicals, like norepinephrine, coursing through our bodies. The result of these physiological changes is that we become more vigilant about our environment, and these can be life-saving. But extreme physiological activity like this over a period of time also wears us down and may have dire consequences. Prolonged stress affects fundamental aspects of our functioning, including concentration, sleep, mood, affect, and state of mind. Fortunately, there is the parasympathetic system to counterbalance sympathetic activity.[7]

The PNS gives us what we need to rest and recover. This parasympathetic side slows the pace of our breathing, deflates our blood pressure, and diverts blood supply to vital organs. Stress hormones are replaced with chemicals like acetylcholine, and we can enjoy that couch potato bliss that arrives alongside deep relaxation. You have probably experienced how listening to music that is familiar and enjoyable can activate the parasympathetic response.

Resilience

It is wonderful to feel the profound repose associated with the PNS. However, it is the balance of SNS and PNS activity that brings stability to our inner workings and contributes to that sense of wellness that we seek.

"Allostasis" is a term that refers to the process of regulation and monitoring of our physiological needs and responses to stress.[8] It is an active and ongoing effort to adjust to the ebb and flow of external conditions that confront us and allocate internal resources to stabilize our reactions. When our ability to cope with difficult circumstances fails, our overworked SNS spins into allostatic overload. We cannot survive in a state of allostatic overload, but fortunately, we are capable of turning off allostatic responses through effective coping mechanisms. Effective achievement of allostasis is one way of defining resilience, something we all covet.

Resilience is another term from the field of physics. Resilience describes how a material compressed by stress bounces back and recovers to its original form. For us humans, resilience means being able to adapt to stress, difficulty, or trauma. Returning to our original status is not possible, but when we learn from our experiences with adversity, we become increasingly more adept at handling future stressors and regulating our nervous system in general. I appreciate the personal story of Elizabeth Gilbert, whose approach to creative living shows us how to uncover the treasures within us, and enhance our resilience, and you might enjoy reading it, too.[9]

Here is where music comes in, helping us grow through distress and anxiety by identifying the creativity that we all have, savoring the sounds that speak to us, and learning how to understand and transform our emotions.

Happiness

I have made the point that you don't have to be healthy to be well. But what about happy? I think we would all like to be happy, and the millions of people who have taken part in corporate trainings, college courses, online learning, and MOOCs (Massive Open Online Courses) on Happiness support this contention. I won't dare to define the term because each of us has our own unique metrics to describe it. However, traditional ways of viewing this concept tend to be related to a person's positivity, life satisfaction, and *affect*—that is, their feelings about their life situation.

On a macro level, the World Happiness Report has quantified it by calculating a happiness quotient for countries around the world.[10] This assessment came about when the United Nations established a Sustainable Development Solutions Network, and policy makers became interested in investigating the wellbeing of its population. Individuals were polled through the Gallup World Poll and asked to evaluate their happiness based on six criteria: freedom, healthy life expectancy, social support, generosity, corruption, and gross domestic product. For the last six years through 2023, Finland has placed first in happiness amongst countries throughout the world.

Penelope Colston decided to unpack this finding by interviewing Finns of diverse backgrounds and professions. In her *New York Times* article, she describes "Sisu," a psychological term that has traditionally been used to represent the grit and determination of the Finnish people.[11] You can imagine that over centuries, surviving frigid winters required immense fortitude and willpower. Now it appears that this trait may be demonstrated in the life satisfaction reported in the poll. Instead of worrying about inconveniences, Finns have reported that they seek self-sufficiency and take every opportunity to enjoy life. It also appears that the Finnish government supports the arts, and many people study musical instruments, sing in ensembles, and attend concerts. This means that artists, musicians, actors, dancers, poets, and various practitioners of performing, contemplative, and cultural arts, find a welcoming home as well as public funding of their ideas.

Being a professor at a college of music in the U.S., I see how musicians struggle to succeed in making a living in the arts. The happiness derived from putting their talent and passion for music to work is heartening to witness. Yet I also see that contentment slip away, when they gird themselves with the grit necessary to prosper in the music industry. Dustin Gee, from the Career Center at Berklee College of Music, reminds students that it takes being open to criticism, a lot of patience, and looking past failure to achieve success. Maintaining happiness along that path requires a strong sense of self and purpose.[12]

In the spirit of full disclosure, I admit that I registered for some classes on happiness myself. Am I happier? Perhaps, but this may be due to the fact that I gained confidence in the practices that I have applied throughout my adult life. I recognized lessons from the fields of mindfulness, cognitive-behavior therapy, third-wave therapies, self-care, and spiritual direction. I found that the strategies I learned were consistent with the music techniques that I apply as a music therapist and teacher, and provided a basis for the success of many of the music-based interventions I recommend in this book. I also realized that while happiness comes and goes, when I feel fulfilled by my work or after creating some music, I experience a multi-layered sense of flourishing. So, if you are seeking happiness now, or more lasting fulfillment, however you define them, feeling the music and seeing the light may be one way to realize this approach to life.

Self-Care

Self-care seems to be a key answer to managing stress. National Public Radio has reported that today's millennials are obsessed with self-care, spending twice as much as baby-boomers did on diets, exercise, and other lifestyle activities marketed as self-help.[13]

In a search for self-care books, I found ten million sources online. Recommendations vary, from taking yoga classes and nature walks to purchasing self-care apps, a certain brand of scented candles, and a massage. Advertising campaigns are replete with solutions to care for yourself, and the pictures look so very inviting.

Lesley Rennis and colleagues surveyed college students about sources of self-care information, and learned that the internet is the most popular source of healthcare and lifestyle recommendations.[14] However, students reported that it was difficult to determine which sources were reliable and credible. One can make the case that there is too much information available—and perhaps, too much misinformation.

Ironically, participation—or rather, lack of participation in self-care regimens—can be a source of stress itself. Common complaints I hear include: "I couldn't make it to the gym this week," "I can't find time for yoga," and "My schedule doesn't allow for anything besides work and housework." There is something very wrong with the contention that "I am *working* on self-care." These statements reflect the attitude that engaging in self-care means that there is one more thing that I have to do, an addition to the burden of demands on my limited time or resources. Developing a feasible self-care plan with reasonable expectations and a sense that "what I can do is enough" may be more effective. But I try to keep my own self-care approach very simple.

To me, self-care is the practice of self-compassion. Yes, I wish to make healthy and joyful choices and find room for activities that enhance my wellness and positivity, like actively performing and composing music. But practicing self-compassion means being patient with myself, forgiving, kind, loving, free from perfectionism and unrealistic goals, and committed to making choices that serve me. In the end, no matter how many exercises I do or minutes of meditation I spend, if I can maintain a compassionate attitude towards myself, especially about what I do and what I don't do, I am caring for myself in the best way possible.

This may sound quite selfish and self-centered. But self-compassion is really about self-awareness and acceptance. Kristin Neff and Christopher Germer detail an approach to mindful self-compassion that is founded in research and clinical experience.[15] They describe yin and yang elements of self-compassion. The yin emphasizes the part of self-compassion that soothes, comforts, and validates who you are. The yang is every bit as important, and includes more active approaches like self-protection (saying "no"), meeting your needs, and motivating yourself from a perspective of love, as opposed to fear. These many aspects of self-compassion can be realized and expressed musically in the creative approach taken in this book.

HOW TO READ AND LISTEN TO THIS BOOK

You are invited to immerse yourself in this book by listening to the music and personal stories told by fellow music lovers, in addition to reading the words on the printed pages.

To access the accompanying audio and video, go to:

www.halleonard.com/mylibrary

...and enter the code found on the first page of this book. This will grant you instant access to every example. Examples with accompanying media are marked with an audio or video icon. Some ebook editions may provide a direct link from these icons, while others may require visiting the associated website.

Audio   **Video**

The first audio file for each chapter is a musical intention for the upcoming material. I suggest that you listen before you begin reading. Then reflect on what you heard and how it made you feel. You can access the music and the stories throughout the chapter in this way, and return to listen again, as you wish.

It will be helpful to have a personal music journal to provide a dedicated space for your reflections and creative ideas, based on the experiences and recommendations in the forthcoming chapters. You can purchase a beautiful, new journal or simply use a notebook or digital folder. If you prefer to take notes on your phone or computer, there are several online tools, like Google Keep or Evernote, for this purpose. I prefer to write in a physical journal because the act of writing is developing new neural pathways in my brain while exercising and challenging my brain.[16] It also gives me more time for reflection and saves my "mistakes," which might come in handy when I reflect on a new question and find the answer there.

You might like to organize your journal with the following headings:

- Reflections on Music
- Reflections on Stories
- Reflections on Exercises
- Potential Lyrics
- Music Playlists
- Music for Special Purposes
- Creative Additions

Music for Wellness: Feel the Music, See the Light is designed to serve as a guidebook for anyone who enjoys music and wishes to make it more a part of their lives, to utilize its gifts in order to feel more whole and well, and to be more creative in influencing our moods and perspectives on life. I hope that you enjoy getting to know the many people who generously shared their original music and their stories, as you contemplate how music can enhance your own wellness.

Feel the Music

What does it mean to feel the music? Part I introduces the impact that music can have on our feelings, emotions, thoughts, moods, souls, and spirits. In these five chapters, we investigate how music can help you feel comfort, motivation, energy, creativity, and spirit. When you listen to each chapter's musical examples and narratives, I hope you will feel the music as the composers and songwriters have. Through them, you can learn and apply a number of strategies to enhance your wellness and wellbeing. Given the diversity of their musical and cultural backgrounds, you will hopefully relate to some of them and see their music as a model for what you can create yourself to meet your own personal needs.

This part investigates the roles that music can play in your life by introducing you to the people who crafted music expressly for this book. Their compositions model how music can contribute to wellness, and in their own voices, they explain the processes and the outcomes of writing this music. You will also read explanations for some of the mechanisms that underly the impact of music, and you can try out some exercises that guide you to apply these concepts to your own needs and interests.

When I wrote much of this book, the world was just beginning to emerge from the isolation of the coronavirus pandemic. Musicians were starting to perform again in public venues, and the technologies that had been connecting us continued bringing access to people who could not otherwise physically participate in community events locally or all over the world. We have been learning lessons from our experiences during that time and utilizing the opportunities that we now have to expand the effects of music on people's wellness and livelihood.

The premise of this book is that music is not simply a pleasant adjunct to a healthy day, but a necessity to keep us focused on the beautiful in life and give our voices a mode of expression that is universal. Read and listen to begin to feel the music and its many potential influences on your life.

CHAPTER 1

Feel the Comfort

1,2

Listen to my musical intention, "Simple Comfort" and my story about its creation.

I am a music therapist, so of course, I brought my playlists to the hospital. I was scheduled for an emergency surgery to remove a cataract, implant a lens, repair a detached and torn retina, take out the vitreous, and inject a gaseous bubble (vitrectomy) in my right eye. I was rapidly losing sight in that eye and was frightened that this operation might not be able to restore my vision. After having endured multiple surgeries for physical challenges other than my eyes, the operating room was a source of fear and panic, and I longed to have something familiar and comforting with me. No one could join me in this sterile space, but I was hoping that it would be possible to listen to music before or after the operation. Fortunately, there is a great deal of research to support the effectiveness of music listening in reducing the stress and anxiety associated with medical procedures.[17]

While in the pre-op area, I was able to listen to music on my relaxing playlist. Simon and Garfunkel provided a "Bridge Over Troubled Water," and Corrine Bailey Rae reminded me to "Put Your Records On." I doused myself with music, focusing on every sound and lyric. I needed to hear the messages like the ones Coldplay's "The Scientist" fed me: "Nobody said it was easy...." Then I went on to purely instrumental sounds, and let the soundtrack from *Departures*, the movie by Yōjirō Takita, flow over me. These are not the latest hits; rather, these selections are like old friends whom I have known well over the years. I can count on them to put me in a deeply relaxed state immediately and effectively. Many say that music provides an escape, when real life is too hard to bear. But for me, music is the magnet that pulls me into the world I create to meet my needs and change my perspective at any moment in time.

Alas, no music was allowed in this operating room, but fortunately, my favorites reside in my head, so I can carry them anywhere. I sang to myself and hummed snippets of soothing sounds and favorite songs. Afterwards, I needed to stay in a head-down position for a while, but I could certainly listen to music, and was prepared with a variety of playlists to meet my every mood.

In this chapter, you will encounter a variety of approaches to music listening for those times when you need to center and find solace. Read about and hear music that has brought about a sense of comfort to others, create a song, and design your own plan for calming and regulating your emotions. As you will be asked to reflect on the experiences suggested here, have your journal handy to explore these more fully.

SOOTHING MUSIC

When we encounter conditions that are unexpected, stressful, or painful, it is common to feel out of control. The circumstances can swirl us into anxiety or depression, agitation or frustration, and a host of other fearful or uncertain moods. Negative thoughts and worries can give rise to thoughts of hopelessness, which in turn, depress our emotions, which then, feed dysfunctional beliefs about our capacity to bounce back. This is a dangerous trajectory that can spiral our emotions in all sorts of perilous directions. We may not even be aware of the cause of our distress—we just feel awful or numb. Uncomfortable feelings may not even be the result of a stressful event, but rather, an overall, unpleasant outlook or sensation.

When we feel this way, we might just need something to intervene and reverse the direction of tumbling emotions and thoughts— anything that can soothe us or help us regulate how we feel. Enter the lullaby! Whether or not you have pleasing memories of being comforted by sweet songs as an infant, lullabies and "songs of kin" have been applied over thousands of years by mothers to console their babies and "lull" them to sleep. "Songs of kin" refer to music chosen by the parent that is part of their culture, history, ethnicity, or other identity. It is this music that carries meaning and connection to one's heritage and roots. There is research to support use of parent-selected lullabies and songs of kin in the neonatal intensive care unit for at-risk infants, and we can learn much about music that comforts from the experiences of parents and babies.[18]

Even though lullabies of different cultures vary, what we think of as a traditional lullaby tends to have certain musical attributes: a slow tempo with a swaying or rocking rhythm; six beats to a measure, emphasizing the first and fourth beat; sung by the mother or with high-pitched instruments, like a music box; and with long, flowing melodies, few surprises, and consonant harmonies, resolving at the end. Yet it is the songs of kin and music that the parent favors that are generally prescribed,[19] whether or not the music is consistent with these elements.

In fact, it is your own musical taste, preferences, and background that will determine which music offers the calm that you seek. Your music may have none of the characteristics listed previously. Instead, your chosen music might simply be a favorite that brings back memories of a familiar place or connects you with a special person. Having a piece or two that tends to relax you will serve you well, when stressors come your way.

Marisabelle is a music therapist at a major medical center, working with people who are in distress, whether from physical pain, discomfort, medical treatment, or poor prognosis.

Listen to Marisabelle's music, and note the effect that it has on you. Marisabelle explains:

> The inspiration behind this soothing music was tied to some of the reflections my patients have shared with me during the receptive music listening experiences I've offered to them. I also drew from what I find to be relaxing, which for me tends to be instrumental music that includes the sound of string instruments, especially violins. This is why I decided to use a bit of violin in the recording. My patients have found soothing fingerstyle guitar playing, which is why I also chose to incorporate this into the music.
>
> My intention for the music is for you to take a moment to connect with yourself and engage in a mindfulness practice. Maybe you want to take a walk to your favorite park while listening to this music or sit in the comfiest spot in your house. Wherever you choose to listen, notice how the music makes you feel. What's your breathing like? Are there certain notes that catch your attention more than others? Does this music remind you of a place, person, or moment you've already experienced?

Listen to Marisabelle's entire story about how she uses music like this in her work as a music therapist.

Note that Marisabelle talks about mindfulness—an act of paying close attention to what is happening in and around you. Throughout this book, you will be encouraged to reflect and notice the impact of music, as you listen and learn about creating conditions that can enhance your wellness. The self-awareness gained from being mindful will serve you well, not simply in regard to music, but to other factors that are affecting your wellbeing.

Pratham is a high school student in India who is in the throes of the exams that will determine his college placement. He has thought about what brings him contentment, particularly when he is experiencing stress. As part of this process, he created a lullaby for a future child, even though he is only a teenager himself. His composition "Rest for Tomorrow" applies the sounds and spirit of his Indian heritage. When he is feeling disconnected or upset, he benefits from listening to this music that is reminiscent of the melodies his mother sang to him. The message is clear: "You were perfect."

Listen to Pratham's music, "Rest for Tomorrow."

Here are the lyrics:

"Rest for Tomorrow" by Pratham

You did well today
Don't care what they say
You were perfect
Let's go rest for tomorrow

Was it a tiring day?
I'm sure it was a busy day
You did well today
But I'm proud every day

You did well today
Don't care what they say
You were perfect
Now let's go rest for tomorrow

Dreams are waiting
For you to go explore
Go see the birds chirping
The mystery man's melody

You are perfect
My little child
Now let's go rest for tomorrow
For tomorrow will come anew

You did well today
Don't care what they say
You were perfect
Now let's go rest for tomorrow

Pratham explains:

> I wrote a lullaby back in 2021, when learning the art of music therapy. From the perspective of a future me as a father singing to my child as I helped them get cozy in their bed, I named this lullaby, "Rest for Tomorrow." What would I want someone to tell me before I slept which would make me happy in general? As a teen in 2023, I understand the everyday pressure of high school, academics, and social life. Tackling these problems, "Rest for Tomorrow" is a hope that my child rests peacefully, having let go of all his past problems, knowing that he has done well, and dreams of that magical realm.
>
> For me, the intention is the key. Knowing what you want to achieve helps you in composing in no time! While writing this song, I distinctly remember jotting down words and phrases that I wanted to hear, like "proud of you" or "perfect." For a song to soothe, it must contain a positive energy that can be absorbed. Therefore, finding that positive energy within yourself, like when I wrote down these words, can allow you as a songwriter to compose a piece that simply works. I often find myself having turned on a voice or video recording and then losing myself to the music. My best music comes from the pieces that I composed and forgot about, because it gives me time to go back to them and reflect. This gap will allow you not only to write better songs but be able to hear them from a fresh perspective and truly experience the calmness of what you have just composed.

Listen to Pratham's entire story.

6

Pratham's hope in composing this music was to relive the experience of being lulled to sleep in his infancy and dream of his future, in order to relieve the tension that he experiences now as an adolescent. He immerses himself in the music that so deeply signifies his roots in India, and attempts to transport listeners to a magical place. He repeats what he wishes to hear: "You were perfect."

While you listened to his music, did you travel somewhere? Did you relate to the message? Did you find the piece soothing?

ASSESS HOW MUSIC AFFECTS YOU

Not everyone has memories of a loving parent who sang lullabies, but all kinds of music can provide that soothing touch. To identify that music for you, you can seek out some with lyrics that carry reassuring messages or instrumentals that seem to put you in the mood that you desire. What one person finds comforting could actually agitate someone else, especially if they are feeling particularly anxious or depressed. Sometimes you know just what will relax you, and sometimes you have no idea. So for now, ignore the structure of the lullaby, and just select a piece that you love. Find a time when you can reduce distractions (if possible!), sit back, and listen not just to the music, but also to your response to the music. Here are some ideas to try:

- Notice the memories and associations that the music elicits and stay there a while.
- Follow your moods as the music flows along.
- Be mindful of what you are thinking about while listening. (Are you able to focus on the music, or are current concerns taking up space in your mind?)
- Check in on what is happening in your body. (Are you breathing at a slower rate, or identifying some kinks or muscle aches?)
- Pay attention to changes in your outlook or overall response to the music.
- Observe sensations of awe, flow, or something indescribable.
- Give yourself time to savor the experience after the piece ends.

It is useful to take notes immediately after you reflect on your listening experience, in order to figure out the impact of this music on your mood. Often, music that you believe to be relaxing is actually exciting and energizing. That's great, but it may or may not represent the sort of music you need to hear when you are in distress.

Note the emotional impact of these pieces and check in again regarding how you feel. Choose another favorite, repeat this exercise, and delight in the impact of this music. You are on your way to creating your own unique playlist for comfort.

FIND YOUR INNER MUSIC

We have been concentrating on the influence of the music you hear on your body, mind, and spirit. Now let's go inward to discover and play with the sounds outside and inside you.

- Notice the sounds around you—there is always ambient sound—and note, if you can, the sound of your breath.

- Follow the path of the air as you inhale. Feel cool air enter your nostrils; imagine it warming through the nasal passages and finally filling your lungs. As you exhale, find the stream of air inside you, and notice how it sounds as it leaves your nose.

- Take several deep breaths and listen. Listen to your own innate music as you notice other sounds of your body. Observe the harmony between your inner rhythm and the natural music of the environment.

- Listen for as long as you like, and then start to listen for sounds that are farther away. Go back and forth between your inner sounds and the environmental sounds you are hearing. Listen for more distant sounds now, and interact with those sounds in some way.

- If you wish, create some new sounds. You can hum, buzz, whistle, or sing a tone. Start softly so that you are still hearing the sounds inside and out. As you generate more energy, allow the sounds you are creating to become louder. You can use your body as a drum, or tap and touch, testing the natural resonance of different parts of your body. Find a way to have these sounds interact with the sounds of your body. If a song comes to mind, sing it out. If you feel like moving, do so in any way you like, and create your own original dance.

- Let your energy guide your music and express how you feel right now. Let it come to a crescendo, and then slowly, only when it is time, let it wind down to the pace that feels just right. Revel in that rhythm—your natural, organic rhythm— and let your music or dance come to rest. Trust your music to play itself out at just the right time.

- Focus on your breath once again. Follow it in and out of your body. Notice its tempo and its rhythm. Find your pulse in your neck or wrist. Listen and compare this rhythm to your breath.

- Pause here to enjoy the rest, and listen carefully to your body's music now. Is the rhythm changing? Did this music express something about your inner self? Did you recognize an inner child or a part of you that hasn't received much attention lately? Enjoy the music of your living body a little longer, and rejoin your daily activities when you are ready. Do you feel a little different? Notice and appreciate the music that is uniquely you.

- Take a few minutes to reflect on the experience in your journal.

You can listen to these instructions here.

7 CREATE YOUR SOOTHING PLAYLIST

You have just mastered an assessment process for identifying the music you need to hear when you are in distress, and to encourage awareness of the natural sounds in and around you. Now think about music that has particular meaning to you—music that has strong ties to:

- pleasant memories from childhood or adolescent years
- milestones, like graduations and weddings
- relationships with loved ones
- concerts and special events
- religious traditions
- vacations and good times
- celebrations and times when you felt comfortable and relaxed

List the songs and selections that you generated here in your journal. Actively listen to and reflect on each, while you surround yourself with this music that says so much about who you are. Your notes will reveal which music might be part of your self-soothing playlist, which pieces fit a different mood, and how this music could help you through a difficult day.

You might like to create your own lists, and you can also defer to some of the streaming services that use algorithms to recommend music, based on your preferences. Spotify, Pandora, Apple Music, Google Play Music, and Amazon Music are some popular applications for developing personal playlists. These can be useful for enriching your compilation by introducing you to new musical possibilities.

If you are already in the habit of generating playlists, think about categorizing them by mood. You might create some playlists that evoke happiness, peace, excitement, stillness, or silliness. Then add some that capture sadness, anger, frustration, or restlessness. In *Manage Your Stress and Pain through Music,*[20] Susan Mandel and I recommend these mood-enhancing playlists:

- **Relaxing music** with familiar, comforting resonances and reassuring messages
- **Attention-focusing music** with strong associations, distinctive rhythms, or affirming lyrics
- **Energizing music** with positive themes and driving beats
- **Sleep-inducing music** with repetitive and deeply peaceful sounds
- **Spiritual music** that is meaningful to you and transcends description

When you practice listening to music and to your own body, mind, and spirit, you are growing in the self-awareness that is necessary to understand your feelings and needs, and ultimately, to provide the self-care that contributes to wellness.

THE ISO PRINCIPLE AND ENTRAINMENT

Often, lullaby-like music is too distinctly different from our current mood to help calm us. In fact, it can have the opposite effect. If you're depressed, downhearted, or simply unmotivated, peppy music might really annoy you. It's so far away from how you feel that it can be quite discomforting or agitating. If you're overwhelmed and can't sit still, the soft, flowing music that you have been listening to might not resonate with your moods, and won't reach you where you are.

When we are out of sorts, for whatever reason, it can be useful to explore our emotions in order to understand and, ultimately, change the way we feel. When we are not in control of surrounding conditions—and are we ever really in control?—we can reflect on our feelings and begin to understand what we need.

Fortunately, we do not have to name our emotions, because music is like an interactive translation app that turns our innate, internal world into soundscapes. A piece of music can bring an instant awareness of our feelings.

Do you ever find yourself saying, "Yes, that's just how I feel!" when you hear a song? That songwriter or composer can express the same sort of sensations that you are encountering, and you feel an immediate connection.

One tried-and-true music therapy strategy for people in distress is based on matching the mood and feelings of the person with a fitting piece of music. Music therapists meet people where they are, and then gradually modulate the musical experience to change how they feel. In 1948, Ira Altshuler coined the term "iso principle"[21] to describe this phenomenon, based on the Greek word, "iso," for equal. Now, scientists use the word "entrainment"[22] to explain the way in which one's physical movements, breath, and emotional responses can synchronize with music that the person hears as it is playing. This allows us to slowly change our feelings with a musical accompaniment that gradually evolves and carries us along an emotional pathway.

You can develop an entrainment/mood manager playlist by first finding a piece of music that matches how you feel when you are in distress. Take a listening bath, as you go through your collections of music from playlists or from your memory bank. Immerse yourself, and take note of how the music makes you feel. Notice how your body and mind react, perhaps even your soul. The musical phrases, harmonies, or rhythms might resonate with your energy, or the song lyrics can say something you didn't even know you were feeling. Maybe the music speaks to you, reflects how you're feeling right now, or has that vibe that meets your energy or natural rhythm. The lyrics might express a message you want to hear or an experience that you are going through.

Take some time to reflect on how you feel while you listen to music you like. Be aware that it might be easy to wallow in music that matches your loneliness, sadness, or nervousness. While acknowledging that your true feelings can be good for you, you don't want to stay there too long. So, the next step is to find music that communicates the way you'd like to feel—hopeful, content, energized?—you decide. What music evokes that mood you're looking for? Those will be the final selections on your mood manager playlist. Next, you fill in the gap between these two with music that is similar to the first piece, and gradually becomes more like the last piece. You can interpret this any way that seems right for you, but see if you can find music that takes you from where you are to where you want to be. Maybe it has a sad vibe but hopeful lyrics, or it's upbeat but has a serious message.

There's your new entrainment playlist to manage and shift your mood! It starts with the music that fits the mood you'd like to change, adds that music in the middle ground, and ends with the music that provides the mood you are seeking.

Samuel is a music therapist from Mexico, currently working in Germany. Samuel is a guitarist and aficionado of jazz, so of course, his playlist has lots of jazz standards, in addition to other beloved music. He created an entrainment playlist, intended to move the listener from a "nervous-to-calm" state.

NERVOUS-TO-CALM PLAYLIST BY SAMUEL

1. "Ascension" Edition 1 (John Coltrane)

2. "Song X" (Pat Metheny, Ornette Coleman)

3. "Caravan" (Duke Ellington)

4. "Island Feeling" (Dave Holland, Zakir Hussain, Chris Potter)

5. "Here's That Rainy Day" (Joe Pass)

6. "My Funny Valentine" (Grant Green)

7. "Naima" (John Coltrane)

8. "Blue in Green" (Miles Davis)

9. "Above the Treetops" (Pat Metheny Group)

10. "The Beauty of Dissolving Portraits" (Ambrose Akinmusire)

Samuel explains how he developed this playlist, with the iso principle and entrainment in mind.

> The challenge in selecting music for this playlist is that the meaning of "nervous" or "peaceful" is subjective. For example, John Coltrane's free jazz music was once described as "hate music" or that he was playing an "angry tenor," which he never understood because the music brought him closer to his own inner peace.
>
> For me, the free jazz movement of John Coltrane and his contemporaries, as reflected in his recording, "Ascension," from this playlist, and the second song from the playlist by Ornette Coleman, "Song X," convey a sense of nervousness that parallels the civil rights movement and other feelings of their epoch. Therefore, I start my playlist with two examples of their music. Notice that depending on my state, I might just play a fragment of "Ascension."
>
> The playlist then moves on to two upbeat tunes, "Caravan" and "Island Feeling." Both songs have a lot of energy but are played in a more organized way as an ensemble. "Caravan" uses sounds and scales that are not common in Western contemporary music, creating a foreign and nervous feeling, while "Island Feeling" takes that energy closer to home, bringing on a groove that gets you moving and changes the energy that you might be feeling.
>
> Next, I introduce a solo guitar piece by the great Joe Pass, which is, for me, the perfect song for the middle of the playlist, as it evokes positive feelings. However, Pass's complex *reharmonizations* (atypical harmonies) and rhythmic energy still connects it to the previous tunes.
>
> The following three songs, "My Funny Valentine," "Naima," and "Blue in Green," return to a combo setting but are now ballads with a depth of feeling in the melody, harmony, and improvisations that creates a peaceful mood for me.
>
> Lastly, the playlist finishes with two compositions that break away from the typical "straight-ahead jazz" language. These are: "Above the Treetops" by Pat Matheny and "The Beauty of Dissolving Portraits" by Ambrose Akinmusire. For

me, bringing it all together and going beyond convention is what feeling peaceful is about. It is about taking all the energy we have and expressing it through art and channeling it to beauty and feelings that go back to the roots of who we are and extend beyond to the cosmos.

Listen to Samuel's entire description of how he developed this entrainment playlist.

8

I enjoy listening to Samuel's favorites in this example, and can often feel my mood shift when I hear pieces that I particularly love. However, Samuel's list is based on his taste and personal listening history. What sort of mood manager playlist would you like to create?

EVEN IN DIRE CIRCUMSTANCES

As I was writing this book in 2023, President Biden announced the end of the coronavirus pandemic in the U.S.[23] Although many experts and members of the general public disagreed that COVID-19 was no longer problematic, this message marked three years of isolation, fear, and bearing the loss of some seven million people worldwide. The aftermath of this global trauma has yet to be felt, but it is clear that it has taken a significant toll on mental and physical health. As we begin to enter a post-pandemic world, or at least learn to live with the virus, we could use some tools to help us cope with this transition.

As a music therapist, I have had the privilege of witnessing the powerful impact of music on individuals experiencing anxiety, pain, and a variety of psychological conditions. Could something as simple as listening to music really help us with re-entry post-pandemic?

At times like these, we have the opportunity to reflect on our experiences and use this wisdom to help ourselves adjust, as well as support others, and contribute to society at large. It may be easier to focus on the many losses, but what about moments of gratitude, meaning, and beauty? We may consider ourselves to be resilient, but are we learning and growing from this experience? This is where engaging with music can help.

COMFORT OF SELF-AFFIRMATION

Emily is training to become a music therapist. She enjoys listening to music she loves, but when she writes music to express her life experience, she adds a visceral layer to the process of finding comfort. In her original, soothing music, she investigates what it takes to re-experience the comfort of home.

Listen to Emily's music, "Home." Here are Emily's lyrics.

9

"Home" by Emily

A whisper screams, "stay"
Stop running away
Stay right here
Stay right here

Clouded mind wants to fly
But I'll choose to stay
I am here
I am here

My tears start flowing
I'm coming home
My breath moves real slowly
Bringing me home
With a hand on my heart
This is me letting go
How'd I get so far
When I'm this close to home

That whisper speaks:
"Feel your feet on the ground
Let earth hold you
Stay right here
Stay right here
I feel my strong bones
They wrap around my soul
I'm here
I am here"

And my tears start flowing
I'm coming home
My breath moves real slowly

It's bringing me home
One hand on my heart
This is me letting go
How'd I get so far
When I'm this close to home
With a hand on my heart
I'm coming home

Emily offers sage advice in the description of creating her song. This authentic expression serves to provide insights about her life and her journey.

> This song was written from a place of wanting to escape the world and my journey back to the present moment which is located at the core of my body, mind, and soul. It is my process of self-soothing and listening to my intuition. My intention with sharing this song is that it can offer an invitation to pause and check in with yourself. It explores the idea of what it means to be centered. The practice of coming back to my center is how I self-soothe, and it starts with simply pausing and taking a breath. For most of my life, I never felt like I could truly trust myself. I looked outside myself for answers to things my body already knew. For so long, it's felt like a battle between the demons in my head and the true essence of who I am. It's so easy to hate yourself when we live in a world that teaches us to have self-doubt and criticism constantly. So many of us have been breathing in the toxicity for our whole lives without understanding that it is poison. This poison was never mine to carry, and I am saying, "No more!" to the voice in my head that tells me I am too much or not enough for this world. There has always been a home inside of me, yet it never felt safe to be there....
>
> Like a meditation, I started to hear the words "I am here" in my head every time I felt myself starting to dissociate. I sat at the piano one day, and the melody came to me attached to those words: "I am here, I am here." This process of repeating those words while playing the music was deeply healing in itself. It all felt right. It felt like an exhale and a relief to simply "be here." The rest of the lyrics came to me over the course of a few months and when the song was almost completed, I felt that I needed to share it with the

world. This feeling of wanting to escape is something that we all feel at some point. It is hard to be alive and present. But in order to be well, we have to stay with ourselves and not ignore our bodies and most importantly, our souls. I deeply feel that if we can be more present with ourselves, we can be more present with others, and when we can truly show up for one another, the world starts to heal, but it all starts with soothing ourselves.

Listen to Emily's entire story.

10

Emily's philosophy teaches us much about finding our home right inside us. Her music communicates a message of comfort to remind us that what we need is sometimes nearby, and sometimes, right here.

MUSIC FOR SLEEP

We have been examining how music can calm us when we are feeling badly. But what about sleep? Is it possible to sleep like a baby if we listen to music before bedtime?

First of all, it is important to note that lack of sleep puts us at risk for disease. When we don't get sufficient sleep, our natural killer (NK) cell activity that defends against viruses and tumors is diminished. So it is no wonder that sleep disturbances are associated with serious diseases, like diabetes and hypertension, as well as chronic pain and obesity. Sleep quality is actually related to life expectancy, so poor sleeping habits are nothing to joke about.[24]

When we sleep well, research confirms that we have better mental health,[25] but you probably know this from personal experience. Sleeping is a complex activity,[26] and sleep meds have lots of side effects, not to mention the possibility of addiction. So it is fortunate that music can provide a safe and effective sleep aid. To improve sleep, listening to music before bed can relax us, distract us from ruminating about the events of the day or worries about tomorrow, and allow us to nod off more easily. Part of this has to do with entrainment—the way that tempo and rhythm of music can become synchronized to our biological processes, such as breathing. Part of it may be that music masks other distractions and negative thoughts. But listening to our soothing music playlists consistently over several weeks has been shown to decrease arousal and condition the relaxation response that facilitates a good night's sleep. There is considerable research evidence to support the use of music for sleep, especially for people with minor sleep problems. One study found that music listening was decidedly more effective than listening to audio books. Yet there is no musical prescription for choice of music. That is completely up to you.[27]

This documentation is quite convincing. But individual sleep patterns, physical and mental health issues, and relationship to music, amongst many other factors, can influence how music works for any one of us. Personally, being a trained musician, I find that I tend to analyze the music that I am hearing, and I give heightened attention to the nuances throughout a piece. So, while I am capable of evoking a deeply relaxed state during the day, I don't find that it necessarily helps me sleep at night. Perhaps this discussion has motivated you to experiment with different forms of music for your sleep hygiene and routine. If you do, don't forget to find a way to turn off your listening device automatically and quietly.

SILENCE

The magnificence of silence will be discussed in future chapters, but the topic is certainly appropriate for our discussion here. Sometimes, the overstimulation of our sound environments necessitates silence, or at least a muffling of external stimuli. Turning off the music and turning inward or outward towards nature may be just the prescription we need. Although there is really no such thing as silence, try limiting environmental sounds for a time, and see what happens. You know the adage, "Silence is golden."[28]

CREATE SOOTHING MUSIC

My sight was still quite distorted when I had a second surgery to remove a cataract in my other eye. I was left with blurry sight for a while, and could not read or do close work of any kind. In addition, my physical activity was limited during this recovery time, so it was challenging to identify a safe way to spend my time. I sauntered over to the piano, where I improvised and eventually composed the piece linked to the beginning of this chapter. I felt so remarkably grateful to have my piano to keep me company and offer me eighty-eight keys to express the comfort that I sought at this time of uncertainty.

Fortunately, my eyes are healing, and I look forward to a nearly full recovery of my eyesight in time. It is ironic that these surgeries reminded me personally of just how feeling the music gave me solace and helped me to see the light.

You might like to listen again to the musical intention that begins this chapter. This was my attempt to bring a comforting start to your reading/listening pleasure through my piano improvisation. Although this piece is original, you might recognize snippets from familiar sources. After recording my music, I heard the beginning of "There Is No Place Like Home" and "Long, Long Ago," then a piece I myself had written before, and finally, the close of the Ukrainian National Anthem. The music in my life's playbook offers a generous supply of themes to infuse into my own musical meanderings. These songs obviously struck a chord of pacifying familiarity for me. So when my intention was to provide the self-soothing that I needed, my fingers seemed almost automatically to play the note patterns that I knew so well.

Indeed, throughout history, thousands of note combinations are repeated in "new" music that steals a few notes here and there, but are fused into something completely different by a new composer. For me, this is one of the joys of creating music. My personal music preferences for certain melodies, harmonic structures, and rhythmic idioms are the building blocks for my creations, whether improvised or composed in a methodical fashion.

I hope that you are inspired to write your own music for soothing yourself and that you see that you are not starting from scratch. If you have no previous musical training, no worries. Your intuition and intention will generate sounds that are authentically and uniquely you! And this music is for you, so let yourself go and get creative. Here are a few ideas for writing your song:

- Find a quiet, comfortable place where you are unlikely to be disturbed.
- Focus on your breath. Inhale and exhale.
- With each exhalation, let out an audible sigh.
- Let the sigh turn into hum.
- With another exhalation, land on one note and hum it softly until you are ready to inhale.

- Think of an intention for your music and put it into a simple word or phrase, e.g., "I am at peace."
- As you arrive at your word or phrase, let the hum slowly turn into the words.
- Begin to chant it by lengthening each word and exaggerating its natural intonation.
- Notice how you are starting to create a pattern.
- Repeat this pattern several times, concentrating on the words.
- Let your breath guide you.
- End your soothing song when it feels right.
- Notice how you feel and reflect on the experience in your journal.

How did it feel to create your own song? Take some notes on your intention, process, and lyrics. If you wish, record your song. This is just the beginning!

CHAPTER 2

Feel the Motivation

Listen to my musical intention for this chapter.

11

My presence in this world has purpose. What I do and who I am can make a difference. I pledge to be present. I pledge to be good. I pledge to bring peace wherever and however I can.

It was the summer of 2021, and the world was just beginning to emerge from many seasons of fear and isolation of the pandemic. I was extremely fortunate and privileged to be in a place where the prevalence and dangers of COVID-19 were fading and restrictions were being lifted. As soon as I was eligible, along with thousands of others, I became vaccinated at Gillette Stadium, the giant football stadium here in Massachusetts. Too bad I wasn't in western Massachusetts to witness the awe of a spontaneous concert by cellist Yo-Yo Ma, a generous offering after his own vaccination. But with this protection, I felt more comfortable gathering with loved ones and resuming some of the social functions that were not possible for over a year.

The pandemic was far from over, with new variants and worrisome statistics coming to light across many countries. Social injustice and political dissention were bleeding into our lives, but I felt that I was at a turning point, with hope that access to vaccines and vigilance to iterations of the virus would allow us to rejoin our communities safely. Maybe then, I could leave the safety of my home and take action. At times of transition like these, we have the opportunity to reflect on our experiences and use this wisdom to help others and contribute to society at large.

In my solitude, however, I felt powerless, overwhelmed by the state of affairs, and despondent about how I could possibly remain resilient and learn how to grow from my experiences, never mind contribute something to reverse the alarming events I witnessed in the massive disorder of the world.

It felt empowering to record this affirmation, but I know that its impact is only lasting when I regularly listen to it and chant along, convincing and reminding myself that I have a purpose. My pledge to myself helps me realize that when I am able, I can act—I will act—and when I feel hopeless, I can hold my intention to do good until a ripe moment unfolds. I can await opportunities to evoke peace, and I can create peace within, as a preposition to true action.

Listen to my story about my intention for this chapter.

12

We have explored how music can be a source of comfort in our lives, especially when we are under stress. Music is also capable of focusing our attention on something meaningful and important. In this way, it can effectively interrupt the flow of negative thoughts, worries, or dysfunctional patterns of thinking. When you can't seem to stop thinking about your fears, losses, or concerns about your future, there is a way through music to disrupt spiraling into pessimism, and instead, send your thoughts whirling into optimism.

This chapter is about how music can motivate, how we can turn an affirmation into a reminder that gets stuck in our heads, how we can empower ourselves, and how we can be inspired to move ahead with our intentions and our mission.

AFFIRMATIONS

You must know that there is some wisdom to affirmations. You can hardly escape seeing them on plaques, greetings, souvenirs, bumper stickers, and advertisements. There are whole books of affirmations for different affinity groups and interests. But lest you think that this craze to utter affirmations is a contemporary gimmick to sell more swag, please note that Havelock Ellis acknowledged the power of such positive intentions and wrote a book on the topic in 1898.[29]

Tara Brach, the author of *Radical Acceptance*,[30] speaks of how our thoughts can all too quickly manifest into despair. While we can be compassionate with others, we are not necessarily kind to ourselves and often feel unworthy of compliments and opportunity. Affirmations can help us realign our thinking, remind us of what we need in a time of need, and reinforce the best part of ourselves. And that may very well get us all through chaotic times and personal crises.

When we feel a sense of threat, reciting personally meaningful and encouraging self-statements has been shown in research studies to enhance positive beliefs and values, decrease our tendency to become defensive, and separate the self from the threat.[31] This means that when we see a threat as something external to ourselves and not so intimately tied to us, we can better cope with it. The impact can be long-lasting and shift our entire perspective. We can develop and hone this valuable resource to reverse patterns of negative thinking and pessimism.

Affirmations often, but not always, begin with "I" and express a positive perspective. These statements are meant to be repeated to ourselves to seal the message into our brains. When we say something over and over, new neuropathways are strengthened, helping us remember them.[32]

Perhaps you have an affirmation, a chant, a prayer, a blessing, or a line of poetry that reminds you of your best attributes or values. Maybe there is a word or phrase that brings to mind a positive intention or hopeful image. What message do you need to hear to set your inner compass to "center" and feel more balanced?

Consider these statements that might resonate with you:

- "I can make it through this."
- "I can hold it together."
- "I can learn something about what is important."
- "Through adversity comes ability."
- "My door is closed, but my heart is open."
- "Peace begins with me."
- "I can't change these conditions, but I can change my perceptions."
- "I don't like it, but I can do it."
- "I am capable of tolerating this."
- "I can find my inner strength as I have before."
- "Here is a chance to show who I am."
- "I see how much I care about others."
- "This too will pass."

Maybe there is a song lyric or title that you love, for example, "like a bridge over troubled water," "don't worry, be happy," "just breathe," or some single words you might relate to, for instance:

- peace
- hope
- love
- now
- open
- accept

When it comes to creating your own affirmations, there are some common pitfalls to avoid. If you are repeating, "I am successful," but you really don't believe it, you can't expect those words to make it happen. Your statements should not deny reality or unfortunate circumstances, but rather affirm what is truly happening or how you are feeling. They can also help to motivate yourself to shift perspectives to something more optimistic. Dr. Lauren Alexander of the Cleveland Clinic suggests that we acknowledge hardship and bring to mind ways that we have gotten through these times before. Emphasizing resilience over denial and conjuring affirmations that challenge negativity may be a winning strategy. But she points out that to be effective, these have to be honest declarations of your own truth.

If you are not in the habit of reciting positive self-statements—and most of us aren't—you may need to practice. We can talk to ourselves in a mirror, but that's not necessary if you feel too self-conscious. Saying these aloud, however, cements those neuropathways in your brain, for future use. While you are thinking positively, don't forget to acknowledge your present less-than-positive experience, so that you don't repress or deny real issues and concerns (for instance, "I am disappointed now, but this might be an opening"). To develop more confidence in your affirmation, you might wish to set up opportunities to act out your wish, like finding a first, small step towards success, showing that inner strength, or reaching out to someone who can reaffirm your potential. Dr. Alexander suggests surrounding yourself with your affirmation(s) on Post-it notes, signs, or iPhone apps, then setting a timer to repeat your statement.[33]

Whatever you choose as your affirmation and however you choose to repeat it, you can break that spiraling down into depression or upward into anxiety when you stop to chant and change your mindset. Whether you write it on a pocket-size piece of paper on your fridge, a banner mounted in your bedroom, or something in between, it can be a reminder that there is another way to think about today's challenge or hardship. To activate more sensory pathways in your brain and strengthen the message, I urge you to consider drawing or painting colorful images on your written note, like a sun, flowers, a smile, peace sign, or whatever your imagination is drawn to.

So, find the words that really speak to you right now. Can you be compassionate with yourself and truly take in this positive message? If you're ready, there's a key role for music in the process.

JINGLES

Surely you are familiar with jingles—those catchy tunes on commercials that tend to get stuck in your head. I'll bet you recall some that are designed by the advertising industry to sell you a product or service. But you can take back this ability of music to infuse your thinking with a message, enhance your motivation, and use it for personal good.

You can create your own personal jingle to motivate yourself with a simple tune. Here are some ways to set your self-statement or word to a melody:

- Use the natural inflection of your statement, and exaggerate it a bit to guide the melody.
- Think of a catchy tune and fit your words to its contour.
- Select a musical theme from a favorite song, and use it to accompany your words.
- Play around and improvise music to suit your statement.
- If you don't want to sing, chant the word or statement on a single note, or in any way that feels right.

I suggest closing your eyes so that you can go inward to take in the impact of your jingle. Repeat the jingle several times until you create the sounds that accentuate your message in your own way. When you find yourself in a state of worry or confusion, sing or chant your jingle and notice how you feel.

THE PURPOSE OF JINGLES

There are many functions that jingles can serve. Let's listen to three examples, composed for different purposes.

Caitlin is a music teacher with a wonderful sense of humor. She created this jingle to start her day with a positive intention. Does it put a smile on your face?

Listen to Caitlin's jingle.

13

Here are the words:

> *Today's a new day, the past's out of sight*
> *Today's a new day, that future is bright*
> *Today's a new day, your truth sets you free*
> *Today's a new day, just gotta do me*
> *'Cause today is a brand new day.*

Caitlin says:

> I believe that many of us come to realize from a very young age that life is full of ups and downs. And while I absolutely embrace feeling every emotion under the sun, there are some days that are extremely difficult to get through. Having a history of mental health issues, including clinical depression, there are times I find it especially difficult to get out of bed and start my day. I had never thought about setting a motto or "words to live by" to a quick personal tune before being introduced to this concept, but the results of doing so have been completely transformative for me....
>
> At the end of the jingle, I decided to add a sort of disclaimer, much like one you might hear at the end of an advertising jingle on TV. I asked my husband to read the disclaimer, because in all honesty, I think he has the perfect voice for voice acting or radio. I think that in adding this, it captured not only my creative side, but the silly, inner child within me which is a massive part of my identity. Andrew reads:
>
> ***Warning:*** *Chanting through repetition of a mantra or jingle can be a form of meditation or deep concentration, intended to bring attention inward and away from negative or dysfunctional thoughts that intrude on a calm mind. Carpe Diem is for everyone. Please ask your nearest spiritual advisor how seizing the day is right for you.*

Listen to Caitlin's delightful story.

You were introduced to Emily's "Home" in chapter 1. Here, her jingle is inspired by nature.

Listen to Emily's jingle.

Here is her text (which she repeats several times).

From the roots of the earth I am held.

Emily states:

> I decided to take a walk, one day, and I started to notice the roots of the trees. I wondered what it looks like underneath the earth, and I started to reflect on how much we as humans can't see on the surface level. These trees have the ability to be grounded and free at the same time. They hold the knowledge that they are connected to the deep truth and wisdom of the earth's soil. At this moment, I realized that the earth is something that has always shown up for me and has never failed to hold my deepest hurt and heal me. I started to repeat the phrase that came to my head: "From the roots of the earth I am held."
>
> This phrase felt comforting to me, and I felt that the more I repeated it, the more I started to believe it. There is power in repetition. There is power in the vulnerability of allowing yourself to be held....
>
> This jingle reminds me that mother earth is always holding me in her sweet arms, even when everything feels like it is falling apart. It reminds me to take deep breaths and feel the ground beneath me. It reminds me that I, too, am divine because I am a part of nature. I am nature. I am deeply loved by the universe and so are you.

Listen to Emily's story.

Marjorie is not a musician, but music is an important part of her life. When she found herself lost on the road and on the verge of a panic attack, she created this jingle spontaneously and chanted it until she reached her destination.

Listen to Marjorie's jingle.

Here are her words, which she repeats several times:

You can do it, You can do it, You can do it, You're almost there.

She describes how music helped.

I was in Los Angeles for a few days visiting family. I am not very familiar with driving around L.A., especially at night. I had driven to my brother's new house on all back roads, and it was an easy drive. When I left my brother's house, it was around 9 P.M., and it was dark and I was alone. I plugged my hotel address into my navigation, and it started to take me on the freeway. There was no safe place to pull over.

It was dark, I was alone, and I was scared. I started feeling more and more anxious. I tend to get very anxious when I am driving and have had panic attacks while driving before, so the fear of the drive became compounded with my fear that I would have a panic attack. Music helps me a lot when I am anxious, especially while I am driving, so I always try to have music on in the car, and when I am very anxious, singing along to the radio helps me the most.

But I could not figure out how to use the radio and navigation simultaneously in the rental car, so I started to sing to myself. I did not think in advance about singing this "jingle" on that dark and stressful drive. I just realized that I needed to sing to keep calm, like I always do, so I started to sing out loud the pep talk I was thinking in my mind: "You can do it, You can do it, You can do it, You're almost there."

I sang it over and over again, and it was working. It kept me distracted, it kept me focused, and it kept me calm. So I kept singing. Telling myself, "You can do it," reminded me that I was capable of the drive. And singing "You're almost there" let me know that I was not going to have to feel stressed for much longer—that there was an end in sight....

I had no idea where I was, but I kept singing, and I kept driving. The song was a distraction, and it was a pep talk to cheer me on and give me the confidence to keep going. And it worked. I didn't stop singing this little "jingle" until I pulled into the hotel driveway. The song kept me calm, and it kept me company. I did not have an anxiety attack or a panic attack. And when I got back to the hotel, I felt proud of myself that I could do it—that I could do the drive and that I was capable of calming myself. The words and the message and the tune are simple but gave me just what I needed at the time. It is important for me to have a plan in case I get an anxiety or panic attack, and to know that I have a tool that can help me cope with and overcome my anxiety.

Now I know that I can start singing a jingle, with this message or even another one, and that I will be able to remain calm and do what I need to do. I think a jingle like this may help others with their anxiety as well. Actually, I think that everyone needs to find their own jingle and the words that give them comfort and bring them peace when they are anxious or discouraged or in pain. Anyone can come up with simple words of encouragement and set these words to their own tune or a familiar tune. We need to be our own cheerleaders and be extra kind and encouraging to ourselves. We can't always count on someone else being there to help us through a tough time. But we always have ourselves. So if we can be our own best friend, we can offer ourselves words of encouragement any time and any place we need them. And if we set these words to music, it magnifies the effect of the words and the amount of comfort we get from them. Music has this amazing ability to lift us and carry us along with it.

Listen to Marjorie's story.

18

I couldn't have said this more eloquently than Marjorie, who found her voice at a moment of need.

These jingles exemplify sources of inspiration, focus of attention, positive diversion, and even active coping tools for extreme distress. It should be no surprise that the repetitive and melodious treatment of an affirmation carries such influence. To find the roots of such a practice, we turn to the mantra.

MANTRA

Yoga came naturally to me. I love the way my body feels after a class, whether it's Ashtanga, Bikram, Hatha, Kripalu, Kundalini, Laughing Yoga, Vinyasa, YogaDance, or practices of other Yoga sutras.[34] I have sampled these and a few more, while avoiding some of the more unusual approaches, like hot yoga, where the room is maintained at a balmy 80 to 100 degrees, and Sound Off yoga, where practitioners listen to their own music through individual headphones. It can be confusing to discriminate between practices that are true to the Hindu roots of yoga, and those that are commercial attempts to lure in more customers.

So, before writing *Integrative Health through Music Therapy*, a book about the integration of ancient healing practices into contemporary Western medicine, I was determined to travel to the home of yoga's roots in India. Just as I was investigating possibilities, I was informed that Russill Paul was about to lead a pilgrimage to Tamil Nadu, where we would reside at an ashram at the southern tip of India. I couldn't believe my luck, as he was the author of a favorite book of mine, *The Yoga of Sound*.[35]

Indeed, I took that trip, and was privileged to enter the inner sanctum of temples to participate in rituals and ceremonies that had been practiced for thousands of years. I learned Nada Yoga, or sound yoga, from Jivamukti yoga, based on the belief that certain vibrations are capable of connecting the outer cosmos with the internal world of the body.[36] I studied with musicians, yogis, and priests, seeking ways to reproduce the ancient formulae for communing with Divine and supernatural forces through mantra.

"Mantra" comes from "manas," Sanskrit for mind, and "tram," meaning protect, free, or move across. As we began chanting the phrases from sacred texts, I could, in fact, feel my mind freeing itself from the endless train of thoughts that I brought with me to India. The repetition of phrases from the Hindu texts absorbed my concentration and brought awareness to the inner massage I was sensing from the reverberation of our chanting.

At the ashram, I settled into lotus position on the floor of the central hall for our first meal, and couldn't believe my ears. The pilgrims were chanting the "Gayatri Mantra" that we would intone three times each day. This meditation to the Savitr or Sun God, found in the *Rig Veda* text, is an homage to the Supreme Creator, and is said to be the mother of all mantras. Although I was unfamiliar with the notes of the chant, I recognized every word as the mantra that my son of blessed memory, Sam, taught me some years before. Mantras have been passed down through generations, whispered into the ear of the son by the father, and chanted at initiation ceremonies. So as a Western feminist, I found it particularly meaningful to be the mother-receiver of this devout practice from my offspring.

I am aware of the precious nature of the mantra, its sanctified place in Hindu ritual and its holy intentions. I also see that the word, mantra, in the Western world has become a catchall for a repeated word or phrase. Indeed, many religions utilize chants from their sacred texts to engage their practitioners in spiritual work and to embody certain passages. So I have struggled to find a way to honor the revered mantra, impart its valuable intentions, and avoid appropriating it for my own purposes. The jingle borrows its physical structure from mantra, but I request that, as you utilize your personal jingles, you think twice before referring to them as mantras, in order to help preserve the dignity and purpose of this sacred practice.

CHANT

Chanting religious texts is central to the rituals, ceremonies, and practices of many religions. It is obvious how chanting and singing together brings unity to a congregation, syncing the words to the same tempos and rhythms, and producing the sounds in unison or harmony. Research has shown that there is a lot more going on. Some of the findings include lower heart rate and blood pressure, decreases in anxiety and depression, enhanced breath control, improved moods, and changes in brain wave activity.[37]

I chant the words of the "Gayatri Mantra" when I have trouble sleeping, in a doctor's office waiting room, and when turbulence is making me jump and shake in an airplane. I sing my son's version[38] (popularized by kirtan singer, Deva Primal), and I can feel his loving presence near me. In a public place, I close my eyes and subvocalize it, focus on it, and let it vibrate my whole self. Sooner than I would think, I am asleep, or called by the nurse, or feeling more stable in that airplane.

POWER SONGS

Like mantras, power songs have their roots in ancient traditions, including the indigenous people who access the Great Spirit and sing in order to hear the truth.[39]

Protest songs are sometimes referred to as power songs that activate social movements. Marches must have a beat to follow and a message that defines its goal or purpose. So, chanting and singing strongly-held beliefs and values generate the energy needed to mobilize and voice indignation. Playing for Change is an example of one international project to unite people in the spirit of changing of the world, through producing music videos that advocate for social issues and fight injustice.[40]

Music sung or chanted in a group is a powerful influence. You can bring that power to your everyday pursuits through finding or creating your own song. A power song doesn't need to be mighty and commanding. It could just as well be peaceful and calm, or simple and sweet, but its message carries the strength to change your perspective. If it transforms your feelings or inspires you to action, consider it your power song.[41]

Mi-Lan is studying music therapy, and she has been investigating contemporary power songs.

Here is Mi-Lan's perspective on power songs:

> I have been intrigued with songs that include messages that empower, uplift, and advocate in some sort of way. We call these power songs. Some of these songs speak directly to the experiences of specific groups of people, whether that be gender identity, sexual orientation, cultural ethnicity, or the generation they were raised in. These songs can even become anthems; the ones that came to my mind were "Run the World" by Beyoncé and "Born This Way" by Lady Gaga.... Some of these songs were less about personal identity and more generally focused on overcoming hardships, like "Rise Up" by Andra Day or "Praying" by Kesha, songs that take a more introspective angle with a focus on vocal melody and lyrics. In either case, listening to a power song makes you feel heard. It makes you feel seen. It gives you something to scream to in the comfort of your bedroom after a hard day or with your best friend during a long car drive. After listening to a power song, it feels like you could do anything....
>
> For the modern power songs, I took to social media to find trending songs like "Truth Hurts" by Lizzo or "Flowers" by Miley Cyrus. I also noticed a pattern of mostly women-identifying artists going viral with power songs—from Doja Cat to Billie Eilish to Meghan Trainor, they all contributed to a larger discography of power songs. As someone who identifies as a woman, I have many of these songs in my back pocket for any day that I'm feeling upset. Whether this

speaks to the use of music as a means of catharsis, or to the rise of a new wave of feminism, or to the effectiveness of our social media algorithm, it's something that I have yet to figure out.... We are in a new digital age, so it's interesting to see how power songs have evolved to fit this.

In this table, Mi-Lan shows the titles of music and the names of artists that exemplify empowerment, according to the themes of personal identity, advocacy, and overcoming hardship.

POWER SONG EXAMPLES

PERSONAL IDENTITY	ADVOCACY	OVERCOMING HARDSHIP
"Thank U, Next" (Ariana Grande)	"Run the World (Girls)" (Beyoncé)	"Fighter" (Christina Aguilera)
"Born This Way" (Lady Gaga)	"This Is America" (Childish Gambino)	"Lose You to Love Me" (Selena Gomez)
"Truth Hurts" (Lizzo)	"Girls Like Girls" (Haley Kiyoko)	"Rise Up" (Andra Day)
"Boss Bitch" (Doja Cat)	"Labour" (Paris Paloma)	"Flowers" (Miley Cyrus)
"Savage" (Megan Thee Stallion)	"All About That Bass" (Meghan Trainor)	"Unstoppable" (Sia)
"My Future" (Billie Eilish)	"Nightmare" (Halsey)	"Happier Than Ever" (Billie Eilish)
"Without Me" (Eminem)	"Q.U.E.E.N." (Janelle Monáe)	"Praying" (Kesha)

🔊 Listen to Mi-Lan's entire commentary.

19

YOUR POWER SONGS

We can all use our creativity to access our inner power, something I prefer to call "empowerment." Each of us has the ability to change how we perceive the world, and when we are surrounded by threats to our wellbeing, we may need an extra ounce of motivation to change—a power song—to remind us of our highest ideals and values, our potential to overcome adversity.

Here are some tips for creating a power song:

- Reflect on a message that can energize you into action.

- Make sure you find time on a regular basis to sing it out, dance to it, hum it, listen to it, accompany it, or play it on an instrument you know or always wanted to learn.

- Record it, harmonize it, embellish it, and find a new way to recreate it in your own way.

- Start a "power club" to share your power music mixes and playlists, and ask your friends and loved ones to contribute their own.

- Listen together with friends or trusted others so that you can process your feelings.

- Find a music therapist to help you process the underlying feelings generated by your power music.

- If you play an instrument, play your heart out or improvise what you want to communicate.

MOTIVATING MUSIC

Bella is a student of music therapy. She enjoys accompanying herself on the guitar, as she develops the messages she wishes to tell herself in songs of love and pride. She wrote a song that soothes, motivates, empowers, and connects the listener with important reminders of what really matters.

Listen to Bella's music.

Check out Bella's lyrics.

20

"I'm Stronger Than I Feel" by Bella

In the past year I have grown
I've learned new things that I've never known

Like gratitude and a lovely attitude
And how to use music to heal
I've learned to love a me that I'm proud of

And I know that I'm stronger than I feel

Here is Bella's story.

> My inspiration for this jingle was truly the progress I have made over the past year. I have found coping skills that work for me and have surrounded myself with people that help to make me the best possible version of myself that I can be. Songwriting especially has taken a huge role in my life, and I am grateful for this as it will only help me to become a better music therapist.
>
> The message I hope to share with this jingle is the power that love and pride in one's self has on the outlook of that person's day, week, and life. This is something that I have learned to be true in my own life. If I start my day reminding myself of these things that I have to be proud of and the reasons why I love myself, it sets a positive tone for that day. I hope that you can also use this form of thinking to help brighten you own life.

Listen to Bella's story.

The power of self-love—now that's empowerment!

21

CODA

There is an interesting research study that examines how adolescents in Canada enhanced their motivation, subjective sense of wellbeing, and global happiness.[42] How did they accomplish this? Well, by listening to music that they considered to be meaningful and pleasurable, of course. What music motivates you, when will you listen to it, and when will you create it? Now might be a good time.

CHAPTER 3

Feel the Energy

Listen to my musical intention, "Bolero," and my description.

Since the pandemic, I have been seeking new sources of energy. After being without live music-making, ensembles, and concerts for so long, I have been wondering: "What does this post-pandemic world look like in the world of music? How could we create a new musical ecosystem that celebrates our common humanity, makes music of all kinds more accessible, and reminds us of what is beautiful and right (or must be righted!) in the world?"

To my delight, the creative spirits of the world have been recording their music through the shared emotional experiences of lockdowns, and in 2020, the pop culture website, TooFab, listed "26 Relatable Songs Written About the Pandemic That Will Cover All Your Quarantine Emotions."[43] In addition, Queen & Adam Lambert revised their very popular "We Are the Champions" to "You Are the Champions," and Gloria Estefan admonished us to "Put On Your Mask!" to replace her hit "Get on Your Feet!" I played these over and over, and laughed and smiled to hear the artists' voices sing out exactly what I was feeling. Somehow knowing that these songwriters understood what I was going through and that they crystallized my very thoughts in something so hip and beautiful transformed my mood. Suddenly, I felt less alone.

Now that we are repositioning ourselves to emerge into a deeply fractured world, I am convinced that music can help us garner the energy we need to forge ahead.

Collectively, if we weave together our imaginative threads of hope for the future, what a colorful quilt we can embroider! What a magnificent soundtrack of emotions we can compose!

What can we learn from this time and from the musical offerings of this time? What will we record for all time? Perhaps now is the time to feel the energy of this moment and communicate it through our music.

AN EMOTIONAL RELEASE

We have been exploring the way that music can both soothe and motivate us, and in so doing, it moves our emotions around and brings our awareness to their tender interplay. Music is also capable of releasing emotions and emancipating the energy that sometimes builds up over time, especially when we neglect to attend to our feelings and moods. You may have witnessed the disarming ability of music to elicit tears, as in an emotional catharsis. You might think that the concept of catharsis originated with Freud's theories of psychoanalysis. However, Aristotle spoke of catharsis as a dramatic purging of feelings when the audience of Greek tragedy reacted to the actors' passion and angst with their own emotional deluge. More recently, it was Josef Breuer's approach to therapy that identified catharsis as a mechanism for bringing the unconscious to conscious awareness through giving it expression. Some current therapies also approach catharsis as an initial means of realizing previously restrained or unfinished self-expression.[44]

At times, without any conscious awareness or intention, those tears stream down when the sympathetic autonomic nervous system (see the introduction for a review) raises its protective arms and signals a fight-or-flight response. The brain's hypothalamus secretes acetylcholine, which activates the lacrimal glands in our eyes. Tear ducts reach saturation and we cry, sometimes uncontrollably. Whether the results are beneficial for our moods is dependent on the personal context related to the situation and the social environment.[45]

A poignant example of catharsis occurred in the aftermath of the fateful flights originating from Boston that crashed into the World Trade Center on September 11, 2001. When employees at Logan Airport organized a service to mourn the deaths of their colleagues and passengers on board, the executive director and CEO of the Massachusetts Port Authority, Virginia Buckingham, reported that while she and other airport administrators had held their emotions in check since the tragedy, it was the singing of "God Bless America" by State Trooper Dan Clark that released tears, sobbing, and a reaching out for comfort and support amongst them.[46] That crying gave excess stress hormones an exit plan, and were liberated in an emotional catharsis. Today, we recognize how the bubbling up and release of repressed emotions leads to psychological health.

The expressive arts therapies (including dance, movement, visual arts, drama, music, and other performing arts) not only value this cathartic function of the arts, but generate and work with catharsis as a means for surveying, and ultimately, regulating and stabilizing emotions.[47] Within the safe container of the therapeutic relationship, those cathartic tears can initiate a healthy exploration of feelings. When amongst others, in a social milieu, they can trigger the reaching out to others who share the emotion of the moment, as they did in the airport hangar. The process unfolds in the service of understanding and managing our emotions, ultimately preserving positive relationships and a sense of wellbeing.

While crying is, no doubt, a powerful emotional outpouring, there are less dramatic and gentler ways that music moves us, mobilizes positive energy, and teaches us how to regulate our emotions.

DRUMMING

Bea is a wife and mother who enjoys playing many instruments, but the drum is particularly precious to her. To enhance her energy, Bea plays the djembe, a goblet-shaped drum of West African origin. Its presence in her life intones wonderful memories. In honor of her father, she drums in the morning, to awaken her energy. Bea speaks about how drumming is a part of her day and her life.

> My father grew up playing the mridangam. It is an ancient drum of ancient origin; it is known as "deva vaadyam" or the "divine instrument." The mridangam is a double-sided drum whose body is usually made using a hollowed piece of jackfruit wood about an inch thick. Each side of the drum is covered in goatskin and has different diameters, so that the same drum can produce both bass and treble tones.
>
> When my father immigrated to the United States, one of the few things he brought with him was his drum. He would often play after a hard day at work. I remember that in the mornings, while he was driving me to school, he would tap the steering wheel or the dashboard of the car in a rhythmic

way, mimicking the way he played his drum, and then sing a tune to get the day started. Once I learned about the "iso principle" in music therapy, my father's actions made sense to me....

I wanted music that would help me get ready to start the day. I wanted to shake off the sleepy feeling, get ready to go, and get revved up for the day.

Listen to Bea's story and a bit of Sri Lankan history.

24

Healing drumming has been practiced in Africa and other nations for centuries,[48] and community drumming is now rising in popularity in the West. Drum circles, traditional drumming, culturally specific drumming ensembles, and mindful drumming are just some of the ways in which people are brought together with the rhythm of the drum. A well-facilitated drumming experience will offer opportunities for exploring creativity through:

- connecting with others in small and large groups
- soloing and playing in ensemble
- leading and following
- composing and improvising
- learning new instruments and modes of expression
- playing music of different cultures
- "conversing" in the language of the drum
- engaging in structured, success-oriented activities
- exploring the emotional impact of drumming
- being part of a community
- feeling vibrations through the body

This shared experience does not require small talk, and you can move to the beat of your own drummer. If drumming is appealing to you, you will probably find some events, classes, and activities in your community. Ask the facilitator about their goals to determine whether this approach meets your interests and needs.

There is some evidence that drumming contributes to good health and wellbeing. When individuals who were seeking mental health services came together to drum, they reported significant decreases in anxiety and depression, as well as improved social resilience and mental wellbeing. By the end of ten weeks of group drumming, these participants' sense of wellness differed significantly from those in a control group who did not experience drumming. Furthermore, immune function in the drummers moved from a pro-inflammatory to an anti-inflammatory profile. Three months later, a follow-up assessment revealed lasting improvements.[49] Other studies have shown that group drumming can reduce stress and systolic blood pressure, and enhance self-esteem.[50] But there is nothing wrong with drumming together just to have fun and meet new people!

SETTING INTENTION

Bea's drumming enlivened her and prepared her for the day ahead. How wonderful to set such an intention.

You, too, can set an intention for your day to get your energy flowing in a healthy direction. Here are some tips:

- When you get up in the morning, take a moment to check in and see how you are feeling in your mind, body, and spirit. Ask yourself the following questions:
  - ¤ "What am I thinking about?"
  - ¤ "How is my body feeling—any kinks or areas of discomfort?" (If so, gently work them out.)
  - ¤ "How am I feeling overall, and is there something else that I sense about today?"
- Close your eyes, and imagine yourself in the best possible light going through your day.
- Ask yourself what would make this the best day possible.
- Consider what you need to enhance your mood today.
- Think of some music that communicates this mood.
- Listen to that music, hum or sing along if feasible, or use your body as percussion to accompany yourself.
- Reflect on how you feel now in your mind, body, and spirit.
- If you found this a positive experience, carry that music around with you, either by singing/humming it or listening to it during the day.

DANCE, MOVEMENT, AND EXERCISE

The piano music that serves as the intention for this chapter is a "bolero." This musical genre, with roots in Cuba, Mexico, and Latin American countries, grew into a quintessential Latin style of love and romance. So, to prepare you for "feeling the energy," my musical introduction had to be in this favorite dance form. Listen again and see if this bolero moves you.

When we say that music moves us, that can refer to being moved physically or emotionally. I have been intrigued with this concept for my whole career, as I believe it holds a key to the influence of music on our moods and emotions. As you know, different music and rhythms elicit diverse movement patterns. As we process rhythm, the motor cortex in our brains is activated. Premotor areas that plan action and the cerebellum that helps us with coordination are also triggered, spurring on our unique movements.

When we are dancing together or in the same space, we begin moving in similar patterns, getting in sync with one another.[51] Cued by the music, and with our shared movements, we mirror each other. Internal vocalization and unconscious awareness result in reflexive muscular expansion and contraction, along with the stretching of muscle "spindles." These spindles are the receptors that communicate with the nervous system and signal kinesthetic responses (internal sensations and movements). When our movement patterns become conscious, they are interpreted and felt, taking into account the relationship between body and self. In her article, "When the Music Moves You," S. E. Pashman says, "Consciously felt movement is emotion."[52]

It's all connected. The Default Mode Network is at work in our brains when we focus inwardly and reflect on memories and emotions. When we hear music we love, there is significant interconnectivity going on in this network, demonstrating a strong bond between music, self-awareness, and empathy.[53] This explanation is a mouthful of technical language, but it helps me understand why we are all so universally responsive to music. If you wish to learn more, there are some fascinating books on the subject.[54]

HEALTH BENEFITS

The benefits of exercise have been well-established, and regular exercise is recommended as part of a healthy lifestyle. But thanks to the portability of personal music devices and smartphones, you can take your music with you and pump up your energy with something peppy and rhythmic. The tempo of the music will set your pace, and you will quickly entrain to the rhythm. You may even find that your energy and stamina are enhanced. In fact, listening to music has been shown to make you feel better, improve your physical performance and efficiency, and decrease your perception of exertion.[55]

When you are listening to the music that you love, you can count on an extra dose of motivation, even when you are spinning at high speed. There is research on cycling that predicts you will cycle further (presumably, more intensely on a stationary bike) with your preferred music, while there is more perceived discomfort with music that you don't particularly like.[56]

There is plenty of research to show the impact of music, movement, and dance in promoting physical activity and sustaining positive health outcomes.[57] Reviews of the literature yield impressive evidence to support the ability of music listening to arouse physiological mechanisms at both the cortical (grey matter in the cerebral cortex) and subcortical levels (deep within the brain).[58] So much is going on under our hoods, as we seek to motivate ourselves to exercise.

But dance, in addition, enhances the aesthetic response and creativity, promoting personal identity and self-esteem, and a sense of belonging. It also teaches us to embody our experiences of the external world, bringing even the most ephemeral sensations into our bodies, thus making them more a real part of us.[59] If that isn't enough, dance improves our *psychomotor* skill—the ability to put our intentions into physical action.

Dance therapists utilize these processes in their work to enhance our health and wellbeing. Dance/movement therapy is a nonverbal, expressive approach that is specifically designed to meet a person's cognitive, social, and emotional needs, often through the process of physical and spiritual integration.[60] It has been found to improve quality of life and interpersonal development, while decreasing depression and anxiety.[61] In more specific clinical settings, dance therapy interventions have been shown to reduce falls in older adults[62] and to improve physical and mental health in persons with pulmonary fibrosis.[63] So think of what it can do for the rest of us.

SPECIAL RHYTHMS

There is one more driving force that deserves attention in our discussion, and that is "groove." Derived from the groove in records that produces sound when the needle slides along that indentation, the phrases, "in the groove" and "groovy" joined other hip vernacular to describe trendy and wonderful things, in addition to music. However, groove is also a technical phenomenon that refers to the nature of music to lead us to tapping our feet and moving in synchrony with a piece of music, as the auditory and motor systems in our brains link up.[64]

Zen is a gifted improviser. He chose a Latin groove as the foundation for his musical contribution to enhance energy. He speaks about the way creating this music served as a catharsis for him. When he visited the beautiful Arnold Arboretum in Boston with the intention to play his guitar, the music arose organically. He describes the process:

> What you hear is this snippet where I am playing something very rhythmically driven; it's quite upbeat. And I think that it's almost like a catharsis, it felt like a release to me—almost welcoming in the summer break with this very upbeat groove. And speaking of groove, I find for me personally, a good rhythm is a way to feel safe in the music. There is almost something trance-inducing about it. It can be hypnotizing if you find a good groove to play along to, and the groove in this I could best describe as a bossa nova, Latin kind of feel. I like this groove because I feel like I don't have to be quite on the beat all the time. It has room for sort of stretching and morphing as the song progresses. There is something very organic about it to me. Also, speaking of organic sounds, you might hear some birds and the wind blowing through some leaves in the background. Something that I love about nature sounds, especially when they are paired with music, is it just feels quiet. It just works somehow, in my opinion.

Listen to Zen's complete introduction and his music.

25,26

This idea of groove in music is also fundamental to a clinical strategy of Neurologic Music Therapy. Rhythmic Auditory Stimulation (RAS) is a richly researched technique, developed for the purpose of aiding people with neurologic conditions, such as Parkinson's disease, stroke, and traumatic brain injury.[65] In RAS, the beat provides a cue that primes us to move at a specific time, resulting in effective rhythmic entrainment. It has been shown to be extremely effective in improving gait to the extent that participants can ambulate with greater speed and stride length, more regular cadence, better posture, and symmetric activation of the legs. So when it's hard to get up in the morning, putting on some music with a strong beat and driving rhythm can coax you to get out of bed, start your quotidian routine on a high note, and even keep your gait even and smooth. Of course, you might want to start with your musical intention for the day to set the mood, and then move with a groove you choose to energize yourself physically.

FIND YOUR INNER RHYTHM

Zen makes it sound easy, but it may not be so simple to find your groove. You have to listen carefully. We used a brief exercise to find our inner music in chapter 1. Let's expand on that process of actively listening with this approach to finding our inner rhythm.

- Take a moment to check in to see how your body is feeling now. Work out any aches or kinks by moving that part of the body gently.
- Check in with your breath by noticing the pace and rhythm of your breathing.
- Notice when thoughts intervene to take your attention away from your breath. Be kind to those thoughts. Let them be, and then turn your focus to the breath. As thoughts come and go (and they will, of course), observe them and be kind to yourself. Just return to the breath.
- Walk around a bit, and notice your natural speed and rhythm.
- Add a natural sound to accompany your walk. You can breathe with a little more intention. You can hum, whistle, or add body percussion.
- Let your body's music continue, and add or subtract elements at will.

27   Listen to my reading of these instructions.

ENTRAINING ENERGY

Just like Samuel's "nervous-to-calm playlist" in chapter 1, Tom created one to entrain a mood change from sad to happy. Tom's background in music theater is reflected in some of his choices.

SAD-TO-HAPPY PLAYLIST BY TOM

1. "People Help the People" (Birdy)
2. "Fix You" (Coldplay)
3. "Begin Again" (The Piano Guys)
4. Theme from *Forrest Gump* (Alan Silvestri)
5. "Rise Up" (Andra Day)
6. "Before the Parade Passes By" (Barbra Streisand)
7. "Waving Through a Window" from the musical *Dear Evan Hansen* (Benj Pasek and Justin Paul)
8. "Feeling Good" (Michael Bublé)
9. "Higher Love" (Whitney Houston)
10. "Wake Me Up Before You Go-Go" (Wham)
11. "Happy" (Pharrell Williams)

Tom explains his process:

> The world has been hard to understand lately, to say the least, and it is easy to lose our grounding, especially when it comes to dealing with sadness. I am very aware that sad and happy are very basic emotions, and we know that there are such complexities within those two words. Within sad and happy, there are a trillion micro-emotions, but we know what both feel like inside, and it is possible by being with music that we can transition from one emotion to another....
>
> I chose Birdy's "People Help the People" to begin because of its nature and sincerity toward humanity—how we all are people struggling. The piano gives breath, offering a chance for us to breathe. Often, using music to support slow

breathing between phrases is helpful for grounding, slowing your heart rate down, and connecting with ourselves.

Listen to Tom's story about creating his playlist.

This is only one example of a playlist intended to entrain your energy from sad to happy. But I hope it will inspire you to consider your favorite songs that reflect both ends of the emotional spectrum to develop your own happiness playlist.

ENERGIZING MUSIC

June is a talented artist who immerses herself in nature and hears its songs. "Wildflower" is her original creation, inspired by the energy of nature's rebirth, and in the hope of galvanizing our own energy, as we listen.

Listen to June's music, "Wildflower."

June's music carries me to magical places of fairies and fantasies. Its delicacy suspends me over a magnificent display of nature's creations and sends me floating over its colorful terrain. How did this music make you feel? Listen again with your eyes closed, and see where it takes you.

Here is June's explanation:

All of nature has a song for me, and I compose by "tuning in" to it. What does a forest sound like? What does a flower sing as it blooms? Breathe deeply and listen.

My music is inspired by the energy and joy of early summer, and seeing wildflowers outdoors feeling the warmth of the sun. I really miss those things during the cold days of winter, and creating this music was my way of capturing those memories to carry their energy with me.

With this music, I hope it will bring you sunlight and uplift your mood and energy. When I feel sad or the sky is gray, this music helps me to remember the place and time when I feel most happy and inspired, the wildflower meadow during summer near my home. I hope when you listen, you feel a sense of excitement and joy, and a radiating light within you!

This piece is a bit unusual in that I wrote it in multiple different time signatures, mainly the odd 7/8. To me, having that odd missing beat creates a stronger drive forward, and also imitates the scurryings of meadow animals, bees, and butterflies, further painting a picture with music. I also wrote it with a Mixolydian-inspired influence [Mixolydian begins and ends on the fifth note of the major scale], as this is the scale I associate with the element of fire which represents energy and motivation. Once the harmony and rhythm were in place, I had to ask myself: "What would the meadow sound like if it could sing? What is the earth saying?" In my mind, I try to tune in and listen while looking at the photos I had taken there, and then note down the melody I heard....

I listen to this music whenever I'm feeling unmotivated or sad, or just need to refresh my energy! I played it on cold days when spring felt far away, and when I closed my eyes while listening, I could imagine a summer day and feel a lightness and warmth in my spirit that refreshes my mind and brings new energy to me. I hope that when you are feeling stagnant, or sad, or blah, that listening to "Wildflower" will bring you new inspiration and refresh your energy so that you can find the beauty and joy in life again.

Listen to June's story.

30

June's Wildflower. Photo by June Westfield

Did you enjoy June's music? Did it take you to the meadow of wildflowers she invoked in her piece? Whether or not it was able to transport you into nature, reflect on your response to this music.

Take some time to think about the music that warms you and the music that replenishes your energy. This is the start to your Energizing Playlist.

THE ENERGY OF BREATH

The source of our life-affirming energy is, of course, the breath. I think we tend to take breathing for granted, because it is involuntary and we don't need any conscious effort to take a breath. Yet there is so much we can learn about ourselves and our emotional states from becoming more aware of our breathing. The word for "breath" is also translated as "universal energy" in Japanese, "spirit" in Latin, "sound" in Hindi, "soul" in Greek and Hebrew, and "universal life force" in Sanskrit. So, breath is clearly more than the inhalations and exhalations that keep us alive.

The way we breathe is intimately tied to our emotions. What happens when you are surprised or shocked? Do you notice a gasp, taking in a quick gulp of breath? When you are relaxed, do you take a longer, deeper breath than usual? When you think about being in love, do you find that you are elongating a sigh of exhalation? Observing and listening to the breath teaches you a good deal about how you are feeling. So it stands to reason that changing the tempo, patterns, and physiology of breathing can actually change our feelings.

There is great spiritual wisdom within the teachings of breathwork, as advanced in the *Yoga Sutras of Patanjali*, written in the second century BCE, and reinterpreted by followers of yogic philosophy and practice over thousands of years.[66] The original text is a guidebook for the paths to enlightenment, "pranayama" being one of the preparatory limbs of yoga. "Prana" is a symbol of life-affirming breath, and "yama" is referred to as moral discipline, so pranayama is meant to discipline the mind through mindful attention to and manipulation of the breath.

In addition to pranayama, there is a tremendous variety of approaches to breathing and breathwork for wellness. There are deep breathing exercises for anxiety and specialized respiratory therapies for asthma. Prepared childbirth methods utilize intentional breathing to focus attention away from labor contractions. Several decades ago, my research with a small sample of women supported the use of music listening in childbirth. Their preferred music served as a cue for deep breathing and breathwork with various rhythmic patterns and increasing tempo throughout labor. Music became an "auditory focal point" for concentration on the breath, and listening to music yielded fewer pain-related responses during labor (observable body tension, shifts in position, and requests for medication).[67] Music added a dimension of familiarity, structure, and celebration to the process of birthing a child.

As for everyday use, a recent study found that a five-minute breath practice could significantly decrease anxiety and invoke a positive mood change, as compared with mindfulness meditation. Three breathwork methods were employed in the research: (1) elongated exhalations (sighs) in a cycle of breathing, (2) inhaling, holding the breath, and exhaling for equal durations, and (3) long inhalations, holding the breath, and short exhalations. Although all of these were effective, the first one with prolonged exhalations had the greatest impact.[68]

No matter how you choose to practice the art of the breath, being mindful of the depth and tempo of your breath and regularly practicing some type of breathwork can contribute to feeling like a breath of fresh air. I like to incorporate music in my personal routine. You might like to try this brief breath practice.

ONE WAY TO BREATHE

- Take a moment to notice your breath. Breathe in through your nose. Breathe out through your mouth. Take your time, and slow the tempo of your breath.
- Think about something you wish to take in now—something you need or desire to instill positive energy. This could be a sense of calm, joy, momentum, drive, forgiveness, or whatever comes to mind.
- Think about what you wish to dispel now—something you don't want or need. It could be nervousness, misery, anger, fatigue, or disappointment.
- With a deep inhalation, absorb the characteristic or feeling you wish to let in to your life. Let the air fill your belly and diaphragm as you inhale.

- With an even deeper exhalation, release the characteristic or feeling you wish to let go of. Feel the air leave your belly and your mouth.
- Repeat this exercise, as you wish.
- Notice how you feel, and reflect on the influence of this practice on your sense of wellbeing.
- Repeat this deep, diaphragmatic breathing as much as you wish, before returning to your routine.

31

Listen to me guide you through this breath practice.

Sometimes, giving yourself time to contemplate how you feel dampens your mood. You might become aware of something joyful or something disturbing. Often, when we engage with our bodies, we identify things that we have been holding inside that we haven't previously been aware of. This can be a natural consequence of going inward and examining our feelings.

If you find that you can't shake negative thoughts and feelings, reach out for help from a friend. If those sensations linger and get in the way of getting on with your day, consider professional help. Taking time to explore the depths of your breath can bring discoveries that you welcome or that you do not desire. Be kind to yourself, honor this experience, and seek the support that you need.

YOUR ENERGIZING PLAYLIST

Whether you choose to drum, dance, or just listen to your favorite energizing music, you can create your own playlist, just as you did for comforting music. Here are some tips:

- Contemplate what an energized state means for you. Do you desire more physical, mental, or spiritual energy? Perhaps all of these?
- Consider what that energized state looks like. Envision how you might show this energy.
- Think about music that communicates the energy that you have just described.
- Review song lyrics for encouraging messages and instrumentals that reflect this level of energy.
- For a potential source of fresh energy, check out some new music.

- Listen and reflect on your selections.
- Ponder whether an entrainment playlist of increasing energy is suitable for your needs and interests.
- Play this music often and let it move you!

The energy of music can be contagious. Consider sharing your energizing playlist with people you know who might need a little boost.

CODA

As the finale for this chapter, listen to the energy of the theme song for A Place to Be, the therapeutic arts organization that Tom built. This music, "Same Sky," speaks about this remarkable village created to welcome community and enhance belonging and hope.

Listen to Tom's music, "Same Sky," and notice how you feel.

32

A person in a chair can live a life that's full
While trying to give back to someone else's soul
No matter if you think
Or look to pretend the rest
For each day that you survive
Feels something like a test

> *Chorus:*
> *When there's just too much to bear*
> *Remember there's one thing we all share*
> *No matter who you are*
> *Or what it takes to thrive*
> *We all live under the same sky*
> *No matter what your challenge*
> *Anyone can try*
> *We all live under the same sky*

Every day we pass someone who could use a little joy
This person comes in many forms
Woman and girl or boy
You can find something good inside of yourself
When you reach out to another
And offer them some to help.
> *(Chorus)*

CHAPTER 4

Feel the Creativity

🔊 **33,34** Listen to my musical intention on the Native American flute and its accompanying description.

Suzanne and Her Native American Flute. Photo by Alan Teperow

I consider myself an "out-of-the-box" thinker, and my aesthetic senses follow suit. My fashion choices tend towards unusual color combinations, asymmetrical patterns, and necklines that have no identifiable name. My hair was cut short on one side and long on the other well before it was in vogue. Now that this is fashionable, I sport only a side part. My preferences for art and jewelry include pieces that defy simple description or derivation. I appreciate one-of-a-kind trinkets and handmade, natural textiles. I like to think of myself as creative in putting myself together every morning.

That said, as soon as I approach my beloved piano, I am an exacting judge. It is only recently that I have been able to lighten up and truly enjoy playing around with themes, like those in my first musical intention for chapter 1. As a classically trained pianist, I have always played by the rules. The technique I honed during thousands of hours of practice demands perfection in the touch and timing of every note and phrase. I used to be terrified at performances because I felt every eye inspecting me and every ear listening for my mistakes—at least, that's how I interpreted the discernment of that daunting audience.

Now when I can lose the crowd and find the zone, I am at my best. When I concentrate fully on the music and interpret the composer's intention with my own spin on it, I feel free at last. This liberty that I am taking with the music ignites my energy and confidence, and I play on with a spark in each note, theme, and eventually, the piece as a whole.

To me, this is creativity—taking some music and making it mine by manipulating its elements in a new way, despite my history of repeated practice and the vast interpretations of others. Yet, creativity is more than assembling colors in a novel fashion or melding my own ideas with someone else's. Creativity has the potential to defy nature, realize our dreams for the future, and challenge society's assumptions. It is the massive power of creativity to birth a new worldview or initiate a systemic cultural revolution that inspires us to use our innate resourcefulness to deliver real socio-cultural transformation. I recall from my studies of the philosophy of science that it takes new ideas that break down existing theories and develop new paradigms that change the way we think.[69] This is creativity at work.

Does it take a creative genius to make us think differently? I believe that if each of us values creativity and the creative process, we are all capable of utilizing our oft-hidden talent to change the way the world works. We are inherently creative beings. When we dare to imagine and act on this impulse, we change our own sense of wellbeing and wellness and take the initiative to live up to our enormous potential.

It is my belief that we can nurture our creativity by being mindful of the everyday opportunities that come our way and by practicing being creative, just as we would approach a sport or musical instrument. We can sharpen our intuition and insights by being mindful and reflective of our daily experiences.[70] Here is another reason I recommend keeping a journal or taking notes on the events that have become routine.

But creativity is not for the timid; it takes courage. So says the author of one of my favorite books, *The Courage to Create*.[71] Rollo May points out that the word "courage" is derived from the French "coeur," or heart. He calls upon us to garner our physical, moral, and social courage to discover and do new things, and ultimately, change the state of affairs. Rollo May sees creativity as an intensely conscious interaction between the individual and the world. When we engage with music and art, or even just respond to it, we gain a new sensibility that changes us. We perceive the ecstasy that originates in a creative act. So, creativity serves us individually, in addition to contributing to new breakthroughs.

BENEFITS OF CREATIVITY

It is obvious that creative engagement is good for us. The professional literature documents that for many, it takes conscientiousness and openness to be creative. In addition, almost anything conducted with the purpose of being creative can bring about a sense of happiness and positivity.[72] In fact, decades of research demonstrate that the creative process ignites positive mood states, motivation, and a forward-looking focus, including happiness.[73] We probably didn't need a largescale investigation to tell us that, but it is nice to see documentation that creativity benefits the creator, as well as the community. I actually think of creativity as a necessary survival skill for living, and a sixth sense with which we perceive the world around us in novel ways. But, rather than a personal talent, it is an ability that we all possess and can use as an agent for change, if we are willing to take on Rollo May's challenge.

PLAYING WITH CREATIVITY

It was the purchase of my flute from a Native American in New Hampshire that allowed me to loosen up. The natural wood and breathy sounds of the instrument drew me into a realm of visceral vibration and resonance. As I listened to the gentle music produced by the man who crafted it, I felt as if he were whispering secrets of his tradition to me personally. I sensed a connection to the land and the indigenous people who used these sounds in their sacred rituals. I vowed to respect the roots of this precious flute and learn the ways of its creator.

I began to initiate my music therapy sessions with improvisations on this Native American flute, finding that it consistently set a mood of quiet contemplation for the listener. Playing the flute for a few minutes also allowed me to center and ground myself, engendering a state of calm. The deep inhalation necessary to gather my breath and the extended exhalation as I breathed into the flute activated my parasympathetic nervous system. Then I was ready to meet my companion on the journey to wellness with an open mind and a relaxed body.

One day, in a rush to arrive at Dana-Farber Cancer Institute where I was conducting research on music therapy for individuals with cancer, I lost the small wooden piece that covered a strategically placed hole in the flute. My magical instrument suddenly lost its magic, and would not produce a sound. Frantically, I sought out information from indigenous communities in New Hampshire, but it was suggested that the man I met was traveling to sell his flutes, and could not be located. Finding no other authentic local option, I resorted to the internet, found a site for Native American flutes in California, and made an urgent call.

I learned that the missing piece was a totem, a sacred tribal symbol. Animal totems were recommended, as power or spirit guides. I could not choose, and said that it was the sound that I was after. I needed the most resonant sound possible for my work as a music therapist. I sent my flute to California to be fitted for a new totem, and two long weeks later, received my cherished instrument, bedecked with its animal guide. It was a bear, a symbol of healing, chosen for me and intended to bring restorative power to the listener—and the player, of course. I conjure up my courage to create through the natural forces of the flute's wood, my life-affirming breath, and the spirit that is imbued with Native American culture and tradition.

Personally, this flute has allowed me to play around musically, something I did not dare to do on the piano in my formative years. I feel liberated, free to experiment, and ready to create. I also feel tremendous responsibility to live up to the bear and its meaningful symbolism. There is something that guides my improvisations that I cannot take credit for. There are the birds that come to mind and the wind that I imagine, and then there is an unintentional direction that the melodies take me. This is the instrument that you heard as the musical intention for this chapter. Did you hear the birds? Did the music take you to a beautiful place in nature? Did it influence your mood? If you were particularly anxious when you listened, remember that it would not necessarily be able to affect you, as much as a piece that more closely matched up with your current state of being. Notice and take some notes.

THE PROCESS OF CREATIVITY

Mihaly Csikszentmihalyi, the brilliant author of *Flow*, also wrote a book on creativity, where he articulated five general aspects of creativity:[74]

- Preparation, immersion, and curiosity about a significant issue
- Incubation, allowing ideas to bubble up without the customary, logical path to solving problems
- Insight, the "eureka" or "aha" moment(s)
- Evaluation, making the decisions necessary to pursue an idea or direction
- Elaboration, the working out of the process, product and implications

This list might imply that there is a direct pathway to creation, but this is far from reality. These steps order themselves in time and take the time they need to gestate. Unpredictable by definition, creativity requires an unplanned course of action with every idea. Yet these steps demonstrate that the process does not occur in a flash, but rather, it advances through a unique evolutionary process.

Professor of Neurology Elkhonon Goldberg unpacks what is happening in the brain by describing two critical processes resulting in creativity. "Hyperfrontality" refers to a particularly active prefrontal cortex during states of wakefulness and attention, particularly when one is seeking goals and solutions. Conversely, "hypofrontality" is the state prominent in sleep, daydreaming, and trance. Temporary or transient hypofrontality is occurring in the creative mind, but it is the "neural dance" in the modulation between both of these states that enhances creative innovation.[75] Of course, the complexity of the brain and the multifaceted nature of creativity add much more to this neurological interplay. However, it is interesting to consider how we cavort between these states in the process of creating new music.

Musical creativity utilizes an abundant toolkit of elements, including melody, harmony, tempo, dynamics, rhythm, timbre, sound structure, form, and function. An endless number of combinations and permutations of musical choices determine how sounds and patterns create a piece of music. In addition, musical training and practice contribute a rich vocabulary for harvesting musical possibilities through the singer's or performer's dexterity, perceptual-motor skills, and learned abilities to produce intended sounds and patterns over time. It is hyperfrontality that calls forth our abilities and prepares us to create music. Then, there is the quiet state that lubricates the process, the hypofrontality that prepares us for making musical decisions. When we analyze creativity like this, it sounds like a daunting task, but sometimes, after gathering our ideas and musical utensils, the process is as simple as entering a room with a guitar.

IN A ROOM WITH A GUITAR

Pratham's process involves a blank sheet of paper, an open mind, and a guitar. His inspiration grows out of his raw emotions and insights. He has a purpose, and is intent on communicating something that others can apply to manage their emotions and energy.

Listen to Pratham's music, "Sama."

35

Pratham describes his creativity:

I once found myself in a room with a guitar in hand, a blank piece of paper in front of me, and a pen. I felt a sense of restlessness within me, an urge to create something new—something that would express the emotions and thoughts that were swirling around in my head.

To start creating, I first took a few deep breaths and closed my eyes, focusing on the rhythm of my breath. I then allowed my fingers to move across the fretboard of the guitar, letting the music flow freely. There was no specific preparation or plan, but rather a willingness to let go of any expectations and allow the creativity to emerge naturally. The inspiration for the song came from the emotions I was feeling at the time, and the desire to express them through music.

My intention for letting my creativity loose was to allow myself to connect with my inner self and let go of any self-doubt or judgment. It had a powerful impact on me, as I felt a sense of liberation and freedom in expressing myself without any constraints. It allowed me to tap into a deep well of emotions and experiences that I may have otherwise suppressed or ignored.

My creative process involved a combination of both automatic writing and deliberate reflection. I allowed the music to guide me and listened carefully to the melodies that emerged. I then reflected on the lyrics, asking myself questions such as "What am I trying to convey?" and "How can I express this emotion in a meaningful way?" The lyrics and melody emerged organically, but the process required a certain level of intention and attention to detail....

I played this recording actually for myself shortly after I finished creating it. It made me feel a sense of pride and accomplishment, as I was able to express myself in a way that felt authentic and meaningful. I observed a sense of calmness and clarity in my mind and body.

And I think that if others were to listen to this music, I would expect them to feel a range of emotions, depending on their own experiences and perspectives. It could potentially affect the listener's energy by helping them connect with their own inner selves and tap into their creativity. For example, if someone is lacking confidence, they could listen to this music as a way to connect with their inner strength and resilience.

Listen to Pratham's story.

36

Pratham's lyrics are self-statements that surfaced when he dove deeply into his emotional state. His reflections and feedback from each line and sound generated a set of messages that he knew he needed to hear. Pratham's title, "Sama," refers to becoming one with someone or something.

"Sama" by Pratham

(Hindi Transliteration)	(Hindi to English Translation)
Mujhko yeh pata hain	*I know that you are here with me*
Ki aap mere saath ho	*I know that you are watching me*
Mujhko yeh pata hain	*Then why do I feel like I am alone?*
Ki aap dekh rahe ho	
	I am just a drop of water in an ocean
Phir kyun mujhe	*A flame of a fire*
Akela, akela, akela, akela	*A grain of sand on this Earth*
Mehsoos hota hain	*I have become one with you*
	I wish I became one with you
Main ek boond hoon samundar ka	*I have become one with you*
Ek aag hoon main jwaala ka	*I wish I became one with you*
Ek ret hoon main dharti ka	
Aap mein sama gaya	
Kaash main sama gaya	
Aap mein sama gaya	
Kaash main sama gaya	
Yeh kaisa brahm hain	
Jo chhoo na paya	
Isse chhoo liya toh	
Ban gayi maya	
Mujhe yeh samjhado	
Zara yeh batado	
Ki kaise samaoon	
Brahm ban jaoon	

INSIDE NATURE

Zen is a guitarist and future music therapist. While Pratham goes inward for inspiration, Zen goes outside and into places of natural beauty to create his compositions. In the process, he invokes the playfulness and innocence of a child's sensibility. He works through his stress, while he builds upon his musical training and ability. He offers two improvisations for us to hear and reflect upon.

Listen to two pieces of Zen's music, "Dream" and "Loom."

37,38

Zen describes his creative process:

> Through some act of a sort of free improvisation, I'm able to actively play out my emotions through my music. And although I might use the term "free improvisation," it's really drawing from my experience as a musician, setting myself certain boundaries, like a certain key, certain chords, or a scale, or maybe even a drone like a sort of anchor. Even though there might be a set of boundaries that I place for myself, these aren't meant to be creatively restrictive, but want to give me a safe space to experiment inside, like a safe musical container. So in a way, I do let my creativity loose, but it's within the bounds that I set for myself....
>
> The piece titled "Dream" was played with the intention of self-soothing during a time of stress.... To achieve this sort of self-soothing effect, I used a major key with lush, colorful voicings. In the piece titled "Loom," I played with the intention of exploring a more complicated side of emotions associated with stress, using a minor key with a more ominous sort of feeling to it....
>
> I use this approach in times of hardship to connect with myself. It allows me to enter a state of mind where I am proud of what I make. I refer to these as a sort of musical meditation; it's a time for self-reflection that I'm developing to become an essential part of my self-care toolkit. I also paint a little bit; I love visual art. I draw parallels between my music and my art.
>
> I improvised both pieces played during midterms week. I was facing a lot of stress and decided to "play out these feelings," from a few different perspectives. The piece titled "Dream" was more from the perspective of a caretaker: I had the intention of self-soothing, easing any feelings of stress. "Loom" was more of an explorative piece into the tougher emotions associated with stress.... It was a way to safely vent what I was going through at the time. Both pieces allowed me a time for reflection, allowed me to notice these emotions and to hear them played out gave me a new perspective on what I was feeling, and I felt a lot more confident in myself after playing these pieces and listening back to them—sort of like a music journal, I guess.

39 Listen to Zen's story.

OUR CREATIVE POTENTIAL

There are no real rules on how to be creative, but there are many books on the subject. *The Art of Noticing: 131 Ways to Spark Creativity, Find Inspiration, and Discover Joy in the Everyday*[76] offers all sorts of scenarios for realizing your creative potential. But the key concepts in this book are all about *noticing*: being alert and mindful of what is happening in each moment, engendering curiosity, taking your time to reflect, and seeking novelty.

To develop musical potential, we might take some tips from Pratham and Zen. Both meditated (inducing hypofrontality) before beginning to improvise. They held intentions to free themselves from self-judgment and criticism. They had faith that the musical themes and patterns would come to them, and harvested their self-confidence to allow themselves to play out with abandon. Pratham took his inspiration from exploring his inner world of experiences, emotions, and intentions and filling his blank paper with notes to self. Zen summoned his carefree youth to welcome his curiosity and sound exploration, surrounding himself in natural beauty. Pratham and Zen have spent hundreds of hours learning their craft and studying music. They remind us that they have invested much energy in states of hyperfrontality that prepare us all for practicing the art of improvisation.

SONGWRITING

Bella was reflecting on the theme of moving forward after loss, and this song "came to her."

Listen to Bella's song.

40

Bella's lyrics reveal her self-awareness and tell her story.

"Without Me" by Bella

I thought that you might have been the one I called home
As it turns out, some people are better off alone
They say that first loves are always the hardest to get over
But if that's true then why don't I feel the need for closure

I left the town that we both were raised on
If not for me then the chance for you to move on
Without me

I had so much growing up to do
But none of that could happen if I was still with you
I mean no disrespect, I hope that you're happier now
And maybe in the future I'll go back and visit our town

I'm so much more now that I can breathe air
But still I hope that you find your happiness there
Without me

You knew me when I didn't know myself
I knew you just like everyone else
Knew you

What are you doing now that I've gone
Do you still miss me, do you miss my songs
Just so you know I think I've finally found my person
I hope you find love too and not just in a bottle of bourbon

I left the town that we both were raised on
Did it for me in the hopes that you could move on
Without me
Without me

Bella describes her process:

> Creating and crafting my songs is so valuable to me, as it allows me to turn my thoughts and words into art. Along with this, creating music gives me the chance to express myself and speak my truth into the universe. This song is one of my favorite works, as it was composed in one sitting. I sang my melody and then found chords to accompany it, adding in comping [accompaniment] patterns after. I then began playing the guitar part and singing whatever words came to mind. I often use audio recording during the writing

process. This way, I do not lose any special lyrics or melodies I've created in the moment. From here, I chose my favorite lyrics and wrote them down....

When I went back and listened to my recording of this song, I felt at ease. When I was writing this song, I felt somewhat sad for the ways in which I've lost my connection to people from my past, yet I also felt thankful for the opportunity to know them. I also went in with the understanding that everything I am now is because of my decision to step away from the safe life I knew and take the risk to find myself, which I believe I have.

I am consistently amazed at the depth of self-understanding and insight that arise out of songwriting. Bella is engaged in a profound self-analysis, moment-by-moment as she plays, sings, and listens. She draws upon the wealth of her experience and the richness of her musicality to create this evocative song.

Listen to Bella's full story about creating this song.

41

SINGING

While animals and objects emit sounds by causing the air to vibrate, it is only the vertebrates—mammals, birds, and fish, for example— who are considered to have a voice. Each of our human voices is distinctive, determined largely by how the breath travels through the vocal folds and entire larynx, lungs, and syrinx in the spinal cord. The voice is, of course, our primary tool of communication, but when it comes to the singing voice, the surrounding culture, society, and mores tend to govern how the voice is used.

Sadly, many of us are self-conscious about our voices and singing. There is a myth that singing should be left to "singers" who have an innate ability to reproduce precomposed songs and/or create melodies that are on pitch and in accordance with rules of rhythm. The talented ones sing on stage and record their offerings; the rest of us may be relegated to listen with our mouths closed, cutting off our own instinctive mode of expression. When we sit and politely applaud as audience members, our natural creative spirits are thwarted. We learn to deny our inherent need for self-expression, and we withhold a vital source of our energy.

Some are privileged to have vocal lessons or coaching that teach breath control, volume production, and how to make the fine auditory discriminations that pinpoint a desired pitch and guide musical phrases. When we learn ways to manipulate our voices to produce the sounds and messages we want to communicate, we can develop the confidence to sing out loud and strong.

Whether or not we have training, we are all singers. So says Tania, a Spanish singer-songwriter who calls herself a musical nomad. Her song, "My Muse," expresses her love for singing and for having music in her life.

Listen to Tania's music.

42

"My Muse" by Tania

> *My muse, you inspire me*
> *Demand me to create*
> *To take responsibility*
> *Through your symphony I get rid of all hate*
> *So tender, I surrender*
> *To your peace and serenity*
> *I give you my all, my legacy*
> *Turning my book of life into prose and poetry*
>
> **Chorus:**
> *Music*
> *Like falling in love for the first time*
> *Butterfly feelings flowing through my rhymes*
> *Music*
> *Like falling in love for the first time*
> *Butterfly feelings flowing through my rhymes*
>
> *I need you when I'm restless*
> *When I cannot cope*
> *You're my addiction, my prescription, my antidote*
> *You kill the poison*
> *You ease the suffering*
> *You numb my pain*
> *My oxygen flowing through my veins*
>
> *(Chorus)*
>
> *You touch my soul, that naked part of me*
> *With your melodic flow, you make me believe*
> *Build a bridge to that broken chord*
> *Revive inside me what's being ignored*
>
> *(Chorus)*

Tania explains:

> All my travels have been motivated by music, whether it was
> for a certain project or to get inspired from other cultures,
> sonorities, and styles, in order to compose and create more
> music. And it all started with my voice. My mom always
> said that the glass windows would shake when I cried as
> a baby. My voice was so profound. It has always been the
> expression of my truth and my feelings, even before I
> could talk. I expressed my pain or whatever I was feeling so
> deeply through my voice that it would turn heads around.
> As a child, when my mom got angry with me, I would start
> singing. It was my way of dealing with the sadness that I felt.
> So I knew early on what music could do for me.
>
> I would always rely on music to understand my purpose.
> This song ["My Muse"] is a love poem to music. I try to
> express this through the tenderness in my voice and tone,
> as if it were a romance. That is my relationship with music—
> ups and downs, intensity, and most of all, love! This music-
> poem was something sweet that I tasted to make me feel
> better—just like candy for a child!
>
> I truly believe that if we have a voice, we can sing. Singing
> is more than expression. Singing is a declaration, an
> announcement of your feelings for others to connect with. It
> can become your voice to express something that you have
> inside, but might not be able to access. Singing goes directly
> to your heart and your heart is your truth.
>
> Anyone can learn how to sing the right notes (with
> practice). But the notes don't matter when you are expressing
> your truth through your voice. It's about connecting to
> the music and connecting to that song inside of you. I am
> following its beat without judging and without thinking that
> I am being judged.
>
> Music has helped me, and still does, to get through difficult
> times both physically and mentally. Music has always been
> and is my go-to, my safe space. I believe the reason I am here
> is to spread love through music. I use it as a medicine and a
> vehicle to transmute feelings. I use it to connect with others
> and with something higher. Music is a unique language, one
> that we can all speak—the language of the universe.

Listen to Tania's story.

43

LEARNING TO SING

Jaime is a dancer. She was sixteen years old when her mother called me seeking singing lessons for her. Other teachers had turned her down, and I was tempted to do the same, when I learned that she was deaf from birth.

When we met, it was very difficult for me to understand Jaime's language. But then she danced, and I saw her unrestrained, liquid energy in a sight more beautiful than a sun shower. The silence in the room was punctuated only by the air displaced by her whooshing movements. I had no idea if it might be possible to teach her to sing, but I wouldn't dare squelch her dream. I started our lesson.

I demonstrated diaphragmatic breathing, inhaling and exhaling slowly, while placing my hand on my protracted belly. We mirrored each other's deep breaths, and remained in sync, practicing for a while. Then I reached my arms high overhead and opened my mouth wide with a yawn. Jaime followed. I quickly bent down, letting my fingers dash through the air until they landed on the floor. My voice followed, and I sang a high-pitched "Ah" and then led a glissando down, letting my voice slide into the lowest sound I could make. We did it together, creating a long and wide sigh, all the way down the scale. I placed two fingers on my throat and Jaime mimicked me. I pulled her fingers to my neck as I throttled on a pitch, until it replicated hers. She changed her pitch, and we lost our bond for the moment. We practiced this way, bobbing up and down for a while and stopping each other at different points in space.

Starting at the floor of Jaime's vocal range, we levitated again until I took Jaime's hands at waist height. She held her pitch, a G above middle C, and I matched her pitch. I placed her fingers on my throat again, and then on hers. She smiled, as she felt our common vibrations. To my surprise, she repeated the pitch, both hands now clutching her throat. I worried that the intensity would strangle herself.

We shook our bodies, loosened up, and sang out "Aah." Jaime steadied her tone, I matched, and we were in unison. We cupped each other's throats and smiled through five seconds of "A-a-a-a-ah." Next, our voices chased our ascending arms with a swooping "Ooh" up to a high note. Somehow, she understood what I was doing, so we moved on to a typical exercise on a single pitch, "Ah, aye, ee, o-o-oh, u-u-u." She repeated the long vowels, and we were communicating in the language of song.

We continued to practice the pitch-matching vibrational exercise, moving on to master two, then three notes in sequence. We rehearsed the melodic patterns of "Do-Re-Mi" from *The Sound of Music*, as I introduced hand signals to cue each note. Five lessons later, Jaime was singing the first three notes to "Doe, a Deer." Somehow, she developed a sense of relative pitch. I could not help her identify the correct starting pitch, but once she began the song, she could create the stepwise pattern of a scale on her own. Over the next few weeks, we returned to breath exercises to improve the timbre of her voice, and her guttural screech was opening into sweet, drawn-out tones.

Jaime mastered my hand signals and eventually, sang all eight notes of the diatonic scale. She learned a wobbly "Happy Birthday," and she overshot the octave by jumping too high. But that's all right. She knew that she went too far. At her next lesson, she was even more excited than usual, as she pressed a leaflet into my hands. It was an announcement of auditions with Up with People. This is a touring group of the country's best young musical stars. I couldn't sanction her auditioning on voice, in addition to dance, but I certainly could not prevent her from trying out. Jaime refined the major scale and then some, and sang, "Doe a Deer" for the audition. A few months later, I received a telephone call from Jaime's mother. She was in. The "Up with People" team must have heard the same music that I did when I first met Jaime.

FINDING YOUR VOICE

I hope that Tania's and Jaime's stories inspire you to develop your voice and listen for your inner voice. By now you have some inkling of how singing can comfort, motivate, and energize you. So, you might like to try some exercises based on Jaime's lessons, get to know more about your unique voice, and see how inspiration can guide you to sing with gusto.

- Find a comfortable place where you can be relatively undisturbed. Stand in this space with a little bend in the knee, if that is easy for you, and look around. If you prefer, you can sit, while you explore the space. Notice details you may not have noticed before. Take a deep breath, and smell the aromas around you. Feel the temperature of the air. Take note of the sounds of this environment.

- Feel the ground with your feet (or your buttocks on your seat), and close your eyes, if you wish to go inward. Imagine a line running from the top of your head, down your spine, into the earth, and all the way down into the center of the planet. Feel this deep centering with the earth. If at any time you feel a little dizzy or weak, open your eyes, find a comfortable spot to sit, and breathe in your accustomed tempo.

- If you are ready to proceed, stand and move your body from side to side in any way that feels good. Come to rest in a relatively balanced point where both sides of your body feel somewhat equal weight. Take a deep breath, fill your belly with life-affirming air, and exhale through your mouth with an audible sound or sigh.

- With the next breath, inhale and exhale to release a wide-mouthed yawn. Reach overhead, look up, open your mouth and let your voice emit a high pitch on "Aah." Stay on that pitch for a few seconds. Then allow your hands to slowly fall towards the ground, bending your knees, as you follow your hands with a glissando of sliding pitches moving down the scale. Hold the low note.

- Take a deep breath in this position, and move your hands and voice upward in a gradual slide up the scale to a comfortable high pitch. Repeat as you wish, changing the tempo of each glissando.

- With the next glissando, find a pitch somewhere in the middle, and sing, "Aah." Repeat, as you notice how this release makes you feel.

- Now play around with the sound, however it feels right. Explore the notes around this tonal center and then try more distant sounds. Let your intuition guide you.

- Take another deep breath and close your eyes, if you prefer. Think about someone or something that inspires you. It can be a loved one, a place in nature, a piece of art, a favorite food, or anything that snaps into your mind. Reflect on this source of inspiration for as long as you like. Then return to the "Aah" sound or pattern you created, and summon your inspiration. Allow your song to evolve at will.

- Record your song, reflect on this experience, and try it again, whenever you wish to exercise your voice.

Listen to my demonstration of this exercise.

44

Did you feel the internal massage that singing offers? Are you inspired to sing another song? I hope that you feel encouraged to develop your voice and perhaps, enroll in vocal classes to learn how to use your voice in healthy and creative ways.

BEING CREATIVE

Learning how to be creative yourself will take some experimentation, exploration, openness, self-compassion, and willingness to take a risk. Here are some thoughts to get you started:

- Be **yourself.** Reflect on what creativity means to you and how you are creative. Then reflect on your intention for being creative.

- Trust **yourself.** Take some risks (propagate courage) to try something new.

- Free **yourself.** Loosen up and let yourself go without judgment.

- **Create** space. Find a place where you can be yourself or surround yourself with inspiring things.

- **Create** time. Reserve a time to devote to a creative project or investigation.

- **Create** opportunity. Consider what conditions can optimize your creativity and make them happen.

- **Cultivate** openness. Your reflections and meditations can bring out your inner wisdom.

- **Cultivate** mindfulness. Attention to the present moment and the act of noticing can inspire you.

- **Cultivate** your creative spirit. Playing with your voice or preferred musical instruments can express things you didn't know you felt.

- **Find** your source of inspiration. Who or what inspires you? It could be a person, natural phenomenon, song, piece of music or art, or really anything.

- **Find** your passion. What ignites your passion? It could be someone or something you love or a social issue you really care about.

- **Find** your medium. Do you want to sing out, improvise, play an instrument, or find a new way to express yourself?

- **Get ready** to record. Have a recording device handy to save any attempts that might be fruitful now or later.

- **Get ready** to have fun. Access the playful child within, a carefree whim, or a readiness to try something.

- **Get ready** to flourish. Feel that sense of pride for having unleashed your creative spirit!

- Sing, dance, play.

- Practice, practice, practice.

Do it, do it more, do it again, and do it differently. Maybe it's time to pack your toolkit with a set of new skills, musical or otherwise, so you have more to play with. Would you like to take up that instrument that you always wanted to play? Would you like to sing in a choir? Would you like to make music listening or activities more a part of your day? What are you waiting for?

CODA

Perhaps creativity can help you as a life skill to solve problems in new ways or bring some fresh perspective to your challenges. Whatever the purpose, discovering your creativity can bring you joy and fulfillment. Give it a try!

CHAPTER 5

Feel the Spirit

Listen to my musical intention on the harmonium and then my story about it.

45,46

Harmonium. Photo by Alan Teperow

I am unapologetically spiritual. I am known professionally for my clinical trials and more recent mechanistic research that attempts to scientifically verify the impact of music, often by controlling variables in a reductionistic manner. What doesn't appear in my medical journal articles, however, is the sense of wonder that punctuates my documentation of the influences of music on human experience.

My technical reports never tell the salient stories. Nor do they reflect the level of contemplation and questioning that I exercise, as I plan a music intervention and analyze the results of my experiments. The most significant findings are often the most poignant and transformative experiences of an individual or group, as a function of engaging with music. This evidence appears in anecdotal accounts that cannot be measured with standardized tests, but they clearly show how listening to a piece of music awakens insights about the past or visions for the future. With active music making, exploration, and creation, there is an even more profound level of engagement that is effusive and indescribable, as the music bonds relationships between strangers engaging with the same music. There is a depth to this encounter that is simply beyond our understanding. Fortunately, it shall remain such, no matter how much research supports its power.

I am often reminded that as a child, when I played piano for members of my family, they would comment that I had a God-given gift, a talent, and musical ability beyond that expected of someone my age. After teachers echoed these remarks, I really didn't know what to make of this compliment, but felt obliged to take them seriously. I realize now that there was an enduring sense of responsibility to study and practice as much as humanly possible in order not to waste this gift from the highest power. I didn't grow up in a religiously observant family, so I had little conception of or belief in God, but I acknowledged that my life's creator endowed me with certain traits, like musical ability. I responded to this obligation, knowing that I had to give something back for that gift. Becoming a music therapist was, thus, more than a career choice, even more than a calling, and more like an agreement with the grantor of my life in this transactional relationship.

I became hungry for more conduits to nourish and express myself, while honing my aptitude. I began to collect instruments from distant lands, savor their sounds, learn their styles, and envision their therapeutic value. I made up for my lack of technique with enhanced intuition and my musical sensibilities, the remnants of my gift.

Now when I play the Native American flute or the harmonium, I am free to communicate beyond the boundaries enforced by the discipline and strict technique I learned at the piano. As I improvise, I am immersed in the invisible waves of intention, within a web of interplay between listener, instrument, and myself. I take a breath.

With the flute, I prepare my message with the deep inhalation and exhalation necessary to fashion a steady sound. I begin the music intentionally at mid-range, so that I can adjust the melody to uplift or relax. I may insert a bird call or a plaintive moan, a familiar phrase or the intonation of a meaningful word. But I will not credit my gift for the music that ensues. Logically, I know that I am grabbing phrases from the storage of musical passages in my memory, but there is also something else guiding the leitmotif that I cannot account for.

With the harmonium, I let this reed organ breathe itself, as I activate the bellows that powers its lungs and produces its nasal music. The harmonium invites me to play familiar melodies on its keyboard. I give the organ agency to welcome me into its resonant realm. You may have encountered this unusual instrument as an accompaniment for yoga class or in a demonstration of ancient scales, the Indian ragas. It is just a petite box, with a few octaves on its keyboard and a bellows giving it life. But you might be as surprised as I was to learn of the origins of this reed organ. Although its current iteration evolved from various instruments, like the mouth organ or Chinese "sheng," it was introduced in Russia, became the "regal" in Germany and the "physharmonica" in Austria, and found another life in France, as the "orgue expressif." After this worldwide tour, it was reimagined in West Bengal, India, to accompany the musicians seated on the floor performing Indian classical music.[77]

So, when I think of the sacred vedas and Sanskrit mantras of India, I can no longer visualize the harmonium accompanying traditions and rituals thousands of years ago. As I pump the bellows and play the miniature keys, I now imagine myself at eye level with the players and chanters in a contemporary ensemble performing classical Indian music, as they celebrate various aspects of religious and secular life. I synchronize the tempo with my breath and allow the instrument to conjure up Sufi whirling dances[78] and call-and-response Kirtan chants[79] from long ago.

While the keyboard of my beloved piano allows me to express myself and communicate the messages I don't know how to say in words, the harmonium provides me with a channel to commune with something more ethereal and unknowable. Perhaps it is the breath of the bellows and the vibrations so alive in the organ that offer this characterization of a living, breathing spirit. Maybe I am just invested in finding a way to touch a world beyond what I can see and hear in front of me.

BECOMING SPIRITUAL

Over the years, I would say that I have become more spiritual. As I encounter "coincidences," ebbs of awe and flow, and the beauty of nature and the arts, my spirit comes alive. I revel in the miracles around me. New life blasts into the world with the cry of a newborn, the blooming of my rhododendrons after five years of hibernation, and the sun alighting every morning. Then, there is the simplicity of the quotidian—awakening to sunshine, a slurp of coffee with just the right amount of milk, and my bus arriving right on time. I used to stand at the bus stop, peeking around the corner, checking my watch, pacing, and worrying that I was going to be late. Now I look right in front of me, savor the multi-fleshed bark of a tree, a weed shooting through the pavement, an insect eating a leaf. A flash of discovery in these "aha" moments lasts the rest of the day.

Maybe it is because I am slowing down, perhaps I am learning to be more observant and mindful, but I know that I actively seek ways to find my spirit throughout the day. The essence of something that I cannot describe comes to me in delight and also in despair. I feel it in my soul, the part of my humanity where I feel things deeply. I feel it in my spirit, when I connect with something beyond what I can sense in the natural world. I love finding joy beneath the mundane, but I am also acutely aware of the suffering. Upon hearing the news of the day, I hold onto the faith that my angst will bring about some action when I can do something to right the world in a tiny way or help someone in need.

I am fortunate to have found a calling in my profession as a music therapist. I feel as though I am exercising the best of my spirit when I lose myself in the act of musical engagement with a person or group. I focus on the unfolding music with my companion(s) on the journey to wellness, and I allow the process to produce its own miracles.

In *The Artist's Way: A Spiritual Path to Higher Creativity*, Julia Cameron offers twelve weekly lessons to spark "spiritual electricity" and open ourselves to our creator's creativity. In the process, Cameron asks us to recover what already exists within every one of us, and explore our sense of safety, identity, power, integrity, possibility, abundance, connection, strength, compassion, self-protection, autonomy, and faith. We explore these paths in a quest to find our inner spirit and the divinity within.[80]

Spirit is often likened to the ineffable. Separate from religion, the word "spirituality" comes from "spirare," the Latin word meaning "to breathe." So it is natural that our life-giving breath is considered not only the source or origin of our existence, but also our connection to creation and the spirit. Breath is, of course, vital for the production of sound and the emergence of communication. The vibrations and sound waves of the breath become our voices and the music "inspired" by our spirits.

MUSIC OF THE SPIRIT

When we go beyond our breath to create music of the spirit, we move into a sphere of another realm. Our intellectual minds seek to understand music, but some would say that it is not meant to be understood. Victor Wooten describes music as a living consciousness that chooses the musicians who play her. His book *The Spirit of Music* speaks to the responsibility of the musician to bring forth this spirit in order to give life to music. Wooten is very clear that we do not create music; rather, we connect with music by pairing up with our instruments, voices, other musicians, and listeners. Only then and there can we find the vibrations and sounds that will become music.[81]

Our relationship with music is akin to the social relationships that are critical elements of wellbeing and wellness. When we forge connections with music, we bond with something transcendent, and this can help us find meaning and purpose in our lives.[82]

Tania was called (received a phone call) to jam with some musicians at a spiritual retreat on the island of Ibiza. She did not know what to expect and felt unprepared. As you listen to this recording, picture yourself near the coastline and see what you hear.

Listen to Tania's music, "Count Your Blessings."

Here are her lyrics.

47

"Count Your Blessings" by Tania

Count your blessings
Count your blessings
Not your fears
Not your tears

But the courage you needed to get here
Not your fears
Not your tears
But the courage you needed to
Count your blessings [x4]

Tania describes her process of improvising amongst a group of musicians she had never met:

> I was completely out of my comfort zone, and I had no other option than to connect with my center—with my truth. That brought me a majestic sense of awe, even entering into a trance state. I was so deeply connected with myself and with the music. And I felt so grateful for being able to guide other people through that journey with us, fusing all our energy and intention. This song was born and created on stage with my fellow musicians who came together in that moment for the first time. In order to connect with everybody in the space, we had to tune into the frequency and vibration that were being produced....
>
> We became merged with nature, animals, earth, ocean, the sky, the moon, the stars, and every single being. This started to enter me into a flow state, feeling deep gratitude for being able to do this and being surrounded by all this peace that is part of us and in us. I then just surrendered to my feelings, my sensations, and that is how this song emerged.
>
> My intention with this music was to use it as a powerful reminder about the importance of focusing on the positivity in our lives, appreciating and celebrating our struggle, our strength, and awe. I believe that life is a blessing or a lesson, and lessons are blessings. So "Count your blessings."

Listen to Tania's explanation.

48

Hélène is a French composer and producer. She uses a modular synthesizer to produce soundscapes for exploration of the senses.

Listen to Hélène's music.

49

> My music is a testimony of the connection I have with the "invisible" that surrounds us. It is often described as intense, spiritual, hypnotic—immersing the listeners in an ocean of sounds that leads to an altered state of consciousness. My work links the past and the present—the memory of abandoned places and the energy they release.
>
> When exploring these places, deep listening is at the center of everything. You are there, silent, in a place you are not supposed to be, where no one is supposed to be, controlling

your breathing, attentive and mindful of your environment. It's a type of meditation on its own. And it already opens a portal, where a lot can be received. It could be described as a type of synesthesia, which is defined by a disturbance of the perception of sensations, through which the subject associates different senses from a single stimulus....

My very first instrument has always been my voice, the first and most natural way to express not only my emotions, but also how I experience this existence. A deep way that transcends words, it is one of the direct accesses for connecting with the creative force, the spiritual realm. When experiencing this state of flow, time does not exist; nothing else exists anymore. You are in the forever present moment—that feeling your heart is going to explode, like you are home again after a very long journey, finally, tears in the eyes, witnessing the beauty and unconditional love that have always been there and accessible—the remembrance of the perfect union, wholeness.

Listen to Hélène's narrative.

50

Tania and Hélène both describe a preparatory step in their creative processes. Tania refers to a trance state, and Hélène calls it a junction moment of deep listening. They both require this "liminal" space in order to access what they need to begin to create. Liminality comes from the Latin for "threshold," and represents an "in-between" state of transition or transformation of identity, as in the case of becoming married after being engaged, or at critical moments in time, like twilight between day and night. Tania moves from being an individual singer to an ensemble member, and Hélène shifts her conscious awareness from external to internal domains. Liminality provides the opportunity to gather the meaning of the moment.[83]

Then there is the "attunement," the process of coming into a state of harmony, as Tania did with the other musicians as well as a merging with nature, and Hélène experienced this when she felt the deep connection to her source. Tania speaks of tuning into the physical frequencies and vibrations around the group, while Hélène senses the "clear vertical energetic movements" from above.

Both musicians are able to articulate the "numinous" space they enter, where mystical or spiritual manifestations of a divine presence or source are felt. They describe "embodying" the experience, as they connect their minds and bodies with their spirits, and communicate what they have gathered through their music. For Tania, this manifests as the melody and lyrics of a song. Hélène creates her music with the modular synthesizer that allows her to choose an almost infinite variety of sounds and tones. In opening their souls and spirits in this process, they are able to share a deeply personal expression and communicate their messages directly to us listeners.

LIFTING THE SPIRIT

Nathan is a composer who writes music for wellness under the name of Chowla Blue. His spiritual music is a call to God or a call from God. Rather than directly summoning God with his voice, he manipulates sounds and patterns of sounds to rouse this call. You can hear the ascent in the musical arpeggios (notes of a chord played in succession) that rise into an ethereal blend of voices and timbres.

Listen to Nathan's music.

51

Nathan explains:

> There are two basic approaches I think I have when creating spiritual music, or spiritual wellness music, or godly music. I'm either focusing on the call to the spirit world or the call to God, or the response or a call from the spirit world, or a call from God. And that call, either way, on either side of that, could be in actual notes played on an instrument, it could be a combination of notes and chords, it could be nature sounds, it could be space sounds. It actually could be the human voice, too. But the sound actually doesn't matter as much as what the sound represents. And at its most basic level, I think the sounds really represent to me my voice calling out to God or God's voice, or the spirit world calling out to me or responding.

> And there are some things involved with that. So, my voice is human, and humans are frail and weak and finite, and we will all expire. God or the spirit world is infinite. And God, him or herself, is omnipotent and omnipresent. And so you have this call and response or call and call or in some combination there that takes place from this weak vessel that is calling out to this divine being or area or existence. In this communion, this dialogue takes place, and this mashup

of humanity and spirituality is really a unique thing for me, and my perspective from creating music for wellness. My call out to the spirit world, in whatever way, shape, or form, is usually communicating a need or a desire or some knowledge I have of what this spirit world exists to be. Even though my needs might be really complex—let's say there's something that's really, really complex that I need, that I need my spirit guide to help me with, and so forth, to me it's complex, but I think to the spirit world, it's really simple....

Can you just help me see something clearly, spirit world or God? Can you help me understand a situation or just in practicality, can you help me be a better person? It seems like a pretty easy thing to do for a being or an existence that's been around for hundreds of billions of years....

One note means so much... That's the way we can actually take the spirituality within us and speak a common language to reach out and touch this spirit world. If you think about it, this one note, that we create to communicate to our spirit world, reaches back the way we are creating it, or the way I created, reaches back hundreds of billions of years to talk to a deity that's been alive that long to reflect the humanity in us...

Listen to more of Nathan's perspectives.

52

While Nathan's musical lines jump upward to accompany our journey to the divine, Gen takes us on an inward expedition. A French Canadian producer and director, Gen is founder of Sound Connective. She invites us to "catch (y)our breath," and take the time to listen in on this communion with the spirit.

Listen to Gen's music.

53

Gen explains her process:

The power of unspoken words that are expressed through melodies, through sounds, through specific arrangements can sometimes go straight to my core and unlock emotions and feelings that I am not able to tap on alone. The elevation that I feel also in my spirit—it's like gates and doors are opening as they are being unlocked by specific musical pieces, sounds, chants. Music seems to establish a direct access to a higher self, allowing me to explore at a level that continues to wow me. I find spiritual music to be incredibly uplifting, especially in the mornings or whenever I need to find inner balance. Mornings can be challenging for me, but taking a moment to immerse myself in peaceful and mindful sounds helps bring a sense of tranquility and clarity to my mind. Personally, I don't resonate with meditation in complete silence. Instead, music acts as a comforting embrace, guiding me through a journey without limitation and granting my mind with a much-needed reset. I believe this could be a wonderful opportunity for you to simply pause and catch your breath. The intention is not to add stress by giving you rules to follow, as we are already stressed enough in our day-to-day life. It is about listening in an organic way, at a moment in time. It's about helping to release tension and allowing the body to fully immerse itself in the music.

Finding a comfortable position, closing your eyes, taking a deep breath, and surrendering to the musical piece can definitely help to create a calming experience, but again, it is up to you to do what feels right.

Listen to Gen's story.

54

Gen surrenders to the music, in the same way that Tania, Hélène, and Nathan allow themselves to open to their spiritual experiences. Gen also feels the connection with her soul within this numinous space. How wonderful it is to start the day with music that uplifts and inspires. Maybe you can, too.

YOUR HIGHER POWER

Caitlin's music is a supplication to God. Her faith and commitment to work through the serious life challenges that confront her are the basis for her very moving song.

Listen to Caitlin's music, "This Sorrow." Caitlin's lyrics are meant to inspire.

55

"This Sorrow" by Caitlin

I'm broken down and tired
Don't know how much more I can take
    (My weary soul)
So where do you go when the darkness settles in
And the fire inside has lost its flame
They say you're there beside me
    (Lay down your load)
But Lord I just can't seem to find my way
    (These chains hold on)
Cause there's this fear and I struggle to let go
So I lift my heart and hands and I pray
    (Help me Jesus)

Chorus:
    O take this sorrow, burden
    I'm falling to my knees
    I'm putting all my trust in You

    My higher power, Father,
    There's good in everything
    But I know that pain is part of life, too

It's hard to understand it
Sometimes I think it's too much to bear
    (Look up, Child)
But I'm reminded of Your love from up above
Doubt fades away when I know You're there
    (I've been set free)
And so I'll walk beside You
'Cause You are the truth that sets me free
And when I think that all hope just might be gone
    (Turn your face to God)
I will lean on the strength You give me
    (Oh sings my soul)

    (Chorus)

Caitlin's perspective on the purpose for creating this song:

> Part of life's beauty is the gift of the full human experience. Without pain, sorrow, and challenges in life, we experience *nothing*. For how could we ever know the beauty of happiness, the strength of overcoming obstacles, the accomplishment of persevering, the knowledge from growth, the power of hope? It's sometimes hard to admit, but the truth is, the tough stuff enriches our lives for the better....
>
> My life has been spinning out of control for some time now. Perhaps this all has been a grand attempt from the universe to help me learn to truly accept the things I cannot change and release my burden. Lately, I'm not sure I have really stopped to listen, let be, and let go. In that way, I think this has been an incredibly insightful and helpful exercise. It has opened up my eyes and allowed me to take a deep breath inward and look around. The ability to surrender in our times of need can be difficult, but the result is always relief. Just like my jingle states, we are the authors of our day, and while we cannot control everything, we can choose our response. This is a time for setting my pride aside, for asking for help, and letting go of the things I cannot control.
>
> While I have written "This Sorrow" in response to a very personal and specific moment in time, these words are for all who are weary or broken, deep in the midst of turmoil, anger, and fear. The chorus is meant to be a meditation you can sing over and over to yourself in those times where life seems too much to bear—where maybe you feel all hope has been lost and there is no turning back. Lift up your burdens to your higher power, whatever or whomever that may be. Know that you are not alone, and that there is a resilience, a strength, a fire deep within you. Sometimes, we just need the help of another to pull us up and out from that pit, to lean on, and share our burden. In time, like the phoenix, you will rise from the ashes and be born anew.

56 Listen to Caitlin's story.

OPENING TO THE SPIRIT OF MUSIC

You have heard stories about evoking the spirit of music and invoking the presence of God. It is time to explore your own spirit in music. I dare not give you guidelines for such an intimate investigation. Like Gen, I would ask you to listen, just listen. Listen to each passing moment. Listen to sound. Listen to silence (I know, there is no silence). Listen to lots of music. Just listen.

Sometimes, I feel like my spirit is hiding under a rock of resistance. I might be afraid to open to possibility or I believe I am unworthy. My beliefs are challenged in an unjust world. My spirit has little or no energy. At these times, I might reach out to a religious leader, service, text, or prayer. I seek a spiritual guide to accompany me on this passage. I look for a community of like-minded others who believe like me and believe in me. I know that, in my heart and soul, I feel deeply, yet my spirit is vulnerable, and unable to access the vitality that allows it to sing.

With music, my spirit has a voice. I don't need to think or reason. I listen. I breathe. I close my eyes and fill the source of my energy with life-affirming air. I find a sound emanating from my center and release it with the next breath. I tap my body in a natural rhythm, move in a dance, or find an instrument to vibrate with my life force.

Will you allow yourself to listen to the source of your inspiration? Have you found the sound of your soul?

PART II

See the Light

Now that we have explored the emotional terrain that music enriches, we are ready to dig a little deeper to excavate the insights that musical journeys uncover. We will see how stopping to reflect and look back at our own histories can allow us to understand the role of music at various stages of our lives. We will see the images and memories elicited by music and how they magnify its impact. We will see the other when we engage in music with and for each other. We will see the self in a new light, as we hear the music and stories that elucidate how music provides a landscape for exploring personal identity. Finally, we see the potential of music to transform the way we see the world.

This set of five chapters is meant to have you integrate the experiences of the composers and create musical opportunities for yourself that are enriching and meaningful to you. Seeing the reflection, the images, the other, the self, and the world allows us to develop a multilayered understanding of the importance of music in our lives, as well as a more profound relationship with music. As we feel, see, and do more with music, we can think beyond our personal needs to those of our communities. After reading and listening, I hope that you will be empowered to engage with music more often and fully, and to enhance your wellness and that of our society at large.

CHAPTER 6

See the Reflection

Listen to my musical intention "Contemplation" and its associated narrative.

57,58

When my eyesight was compromised, I had to slow my steps, notice any obstacles, and move forward gingerly. Now that I am seeing more clearly, I can see how taking those extra seconds served not only my safe mobility, but my wellbeing in general. For many people, a change in their health status, an unfortunate accident, or unbidden trauma changes the way they see the world. They may become more grateful for being able to live every day and enjoy everyday things. They might find that they savor moments of joy or peace more fervently. They can be more mindful about what they experience every moment, instead of forging ahead to what is coming next. I would like to think that I am one of those people, and not just because of changes in the way I see. Becoming more thankful and appreciative, savoring pleasantries, and being mindful makes me feel better.

Recently, a friend celebrated her eightieth birthday. She had undergone several serious illnesses and painful treatments, and never thought she would live that long. On this special occasion, she sent all of her dear friends handmade greeting cards that expressed gratitude for having that person in her life. This is how she expressed what turning eighty meant to her, and she made it special for me, too. When she insisted on hosting her own birthday party, I carried my Native American flute into her garden and improvised, while a group of her friends savored our sacred bond of friendship, and then meditated on the wonder that brought us together. When we show gratitude with generosity, we acquire a wealth of goodness for ourselves and others.

When feeling and showing gratitude, we focus on the positive. "Look on the bright side" and "Find the silver lining" are slick adages we might like to live by. But it is not always easy or even appropriate to maintain an affirmative attitude throughout a difficult situation. We may need to solve an immediate problem, attend to an illness, or take action to remove ourselves or others from danger first. Processing our emotions may certainly be indicated, but when we reflect back on these times, we can discover superpowers in ourselves that helped us make it through challenging times. We can recognize the character traits and coping strategies that we foraged for, uncovered, and utilized. We unpack our toolkits and find our abilities and strengths.

Savoring those times when we are able to find optimism or hidden value in an otherwise arduous situation provides a fertile opportunity to see the resources that we bring to life. Savoring the little things—those details we have overlooked—helps us find beauty and greatness in our surroundings. Savoring every precious moment with mindful attention brings us closer to awe and amazement in our natural world and within ourselves.

To what will we give our attention today? It might be easier to maintain the status quo and wallow in a complacent mood than to change our routine and start a new ritual. But in devising an alternative plan for the day ahead of us, with a little help from our creative spirit, we can reframe our thinking, change our intentions, and make the day ahead a little better.

So catch your breath. Inhale deeply and exhale a sonorous noise to trumpet a new beginning. Part I asked you to feel the comfort, motivation, energy, creativity, and spirit of music. Now we dive below the surface to see the light, the insights gained from these and more functions of music.

It all starts with reflection. When we reflect, we find a mirror for our feelings, emotions, and intentions that illustrates what resides within us. Then we can manifest the gratitude and awe that we quarried, and sing in praise of these gifts. In this chapter, we meet some creative spirits who transcend difficult times through their musical encounters and use music as a source of gratitude and awe.

YOUR MUSICAL AUTOBIOGRAPHY

Let's begin with contemplating the role of music throughout your life. When you remember the paths you took that have enabled you to arrive where you are today, I wonder what music has accompanied this journey. When you think about critical times in your life or mileposts that pointed you in a different direction or onto a whole new road, perhaps there was a song or two that guided you along your way or resonated with your emotional experience.

When you consider the music associated with highlights and stages of your life, you are constructing a musical autobiography. The resulting discography will include music that carries particular meaning and is associated with parts of you that you may have forgotten or ignored. It should also remind you of music that commemorated special times, passages, and key events. This listing will comprise your autobiographical playlist.

The process of rediscovering this music may offer an opportunity to reflect on the experiences and events that shaped who you are today. So I think you will want to keep your journal or notebook handy, as you review your life and recall a particular piece of music that you wish to hear (or sing/play) again. Alternatively, you can add these musical selections directly to your existing playlists on platforms or streaming services, like Spotify, YouTube, Amazon Music, etc. Here are some prompts for your journey down memory lane and some examples to contemplate:

- Think of music that carries fond memories at different times in your life:
  - Childhood
  - Adolescence
  - Emerging adulthood
  - Mid adulthood
  - Later adulthood (if you're there)
- Return to milestones in your development and identify music that is associated with good times:
  - Birthdays and anniversaries
  - Developing relationships (friendship, engagement, marriage, first dance)
  - Life passages

- ¤ Religious rituals and ceremonies
- ¤ Concerts, events, movies
- ¤ Epiphanies and insights about choice points
- ¤ Lessons learned
- ¤ Travels

- Contemplate aspects of daily life or routines where music has played a positive role. Identify the music that accompanies:
  - ¤ Getting going in the morning
  - ¤ Preparing for the day
  - ¤ Preparing for meditation
  - ¤ Doing household or daily living tasks
  - ¤ Eating
  - ¤ Traveling to work, school, or play
  - ¤ Exercising
  - ¤ Dancing
  - ¤ Watching films and attending cultural events
  - ¤ Participating in religious services or cultural rituals
  - ¤ Dealing with stress or pain
  - ¤ Enjoying nature
  - ¤ Enjoying free time
  - ¤ Chilling out at the end of the day
  - ¤ Getting ready to sleep

- Listen to each piece of music as you reflect on:
  - ¤ How it makes you feel
  - ¤ What thoughts and memories are going through your mind
  - ¤ How your breath and sensations in your body change
  - ¤ How your soul and spirit are responding

- Listen again to relive some of these times in your life:
  - ¤ Feel the sensations that you felt at this time
  - ¤ Put yourself back in time and savor the good feelings
  - ¤ Recall the venue and explore it in your mind's eye
  - ¤ Experience the sensations of this time/place (temperature of the air, visual details and colors, smells)

- Add selections to your existing or new music playlists for different emotional effects. Categorize as you wish, but here are some options for organizing your music:
  - ¤ Relaxing, attention-focusing, energizing, sleep-inducing, and spiritual playlists
  - ¤ Entrainment/mood manager playlists that take you from current to desired state
  - ¤ Music sorted by different moods (content, relaxed, motivated, energized, contemplative, passionate)
  - ¤ Music for different times of day (morning boost, prep for/transition from work, evening rest)
  - ¤ Music for different functions (exercise, study, housework, traffic, ritual, prayer, meditation, sleep)
- Interact actively with the music by:
  - ¤ Humming or singing
  - ¤ Playing along with body percussion or musical instruments
  - ¤ Moving or dancing to it
  - ¤ Writing down your story
  - ¤ Drawing, painting, or doodling some art work
  - ¤ Sharing playlists with someone
  - ¤ Ending with silent contemplation of the impact of this music

Now you have a soundtrack for your life's story. Whatever you experienced in taking this personal inventory, reflecting on your life can bring up pivotal moments that deserve more attention or events that you prefer to forget. Be sure to call upon others to accompany you in debriefing and help you hold onto positive and empowering elements of this exploration. While going back in time can be a fruitful and enjoyable endeavor, music carries significant emotional content. So if you find yourself feeling uncomfortable, bring your attention to more positive aspects that you unearthed, and consider seeking professional assistance to support a healthy process of discovery.

As new experiences add meaning to your life, new music that you hear or are exposed to can augment your playlists as well as your individual insights. Let the playlists take any shape you wish and apply them when you want to evoke a particular mood or change the way you feel.

While the purpose of this exercise is to enhance and create new playlists for your wellness, particularly in improving your mood, it may also motivate you to highlight your life's story through writing song lyrics or instrumental music inspired by significant moments. Remember that you can always refer back to your notes when your creative spirit is ready to reveal itself!

PLAYLISTS FOR WELLNESS

As you have already surmised, there are many ways to generate and organize playlists for wellness. Fran and Marisabelle have disparate approaches to creating theirs.

Fran describes her process here:

My "playlist" contains over a million songs—that's no exaggeration, nope, for it's not a playlist of digital tracks that one stores on a mobile device.... Selections, well, they are from myriad musical genres that have shaped my life since I was born in Brooklyn, New York, many decades ago. Music was always playing in my home. My father, an Italian immigrant, played Italian opera; my mother loved big band music and American Songbook artists. At church, I was enveloped by the meditative glory of Gregorian chants. Then in came the dawn of rock 'n' roll: doo-wop, Elvis, the '60s, the British Invasion, classical music, the Blazers—my all-girl rock band of two! Disco, jazz....

So you see, music has always been vital to my life's work. I require it at the beginning, middle, and end of every day. Operating instructions for this playlist are similar to the digital kind, only my device doesn't need batteries or internet connection and is on tap 24/7. It works two ways: I either seek music when I want to express a feeling or if I require a mood "treatment." Selections could be vocal (if I need to hear a singer's voice, like Nat King Cole) or maybe an instrumental, even the calming sounds of nature.

I will then choose from a vast collection of CDs that I have, or if I feel like playing piano, I'll reach to the mountains of song folios that I have....

When I'm feeling anxious, for instance, well, I might reach for Johann Sebastian Bach's *Brandenburg Concerto No. 3 in*

G Major or Verdi's "Overture" to *La Traviata*. The symmetry of Bach always calms and cheers me. When a blast of energy is needed (which is most mornings for me), I play Queen's "Don't Stop Me Now," an exuberant, confidence-building song. When feeling longing, I might turn to a torch song like, "The Man I Love" by Ella Fitzgerald, or an operatic aria, such as "Che Gelida Manina."

At times, I feel the music within reaches out to play *me*, knowing exactly what I need for the day—these are the times I wake up aching to hear a long-forgotten melody or a certain voice or the timbre of a certain instrument. Songs not only conjure up specific memories, but often miraculously recreate for me the actual physical/mental feelings of a certain age. That doo-wop song, "In the Still of the Night," sung by the Five Satins, for example, makes me feel the self-conscious and awkward teenager enjoying her first kiss with Johnny M. So let the music play on, and may it never stop!

Listen to Fran's narrative.

59 Marisabelle is a music therapist who works with hospitalized adults and adolescents. She has found that collections of music, as in the mood manager playlist she shares here, help people process their feelings and work toward emotional wellness. This "Sluggish-to-Energized" entrainment playlist for young adults includes songs that were popular at the time and were chosen for their emotive content. Marisabelle explains:

The initial four songs chosen for this playlist may help in providing the comfort someone needs when noticing that they are not feeling well, are lacking energy, and need a way to express those feelings. With the song "Bittersweet," you can start to sense how you may be shifting to a more energized mood, as you listen to this playlist. Following this song, "Sunday Best" comes in with more liveliness.... This is a good reminder that even though challenges may come up in life, we can still have a day filled with goodness. I think it's on us to decide how much light we may want to shed on that challenge and let it consume our thoughts and mood. The final three songs after "Sunday Best" are quite up-tempo and can have you dancing along to the music without you even noticing. When you dance, you have energy!

Listen to Marisabelle's commentary and see her playlist.

60

"SLUGGISH-TO-ENERGIZED PLAYLIST" BY MARISABELLE

1. "I'm Not OK" (H.E.R.)

2. "Moral of the Story" (Ashe)

3. "Someone You Loved" (Lewis Capaldi)

4. "Making Do" (Lake Street Dive)

5. "Bittersweet" (Lianne La Havas)

6. "Underdog" (Alicia Keys)

7. "Sunday Best" (Surfaces)

8. "Backyard Boy" (Claire Rosinkranz)

9. "Dynamite" (BTS)

10. "Rain on Me" (Lady Gaga, Ariana Grande)

What will your playlists look like? Obviously, they can be as structured and specific as you like, or you can play as you go and discover new songs and pieces of music that you will want to replay and re-experience.

MUSIC AS A COPING MECHANISM

Now that you have playlists amongst your musical resources, you can investigate how you wish to use them in daily life. In *Music Asylums: Wellbeing Through Music in Everyday Life*, Tia DeNora discusses how music helps us create a "room of our own."[84] We can remove ourselves from the vicissitudes of life by plugging into music and building an asylum far away from the trouble or disorder surrounding us. Alternatively, we can refurnish the space where music takes us, engaging with the music and our environment. To me, this means choosing music that adorns us with thoughts and feelings that weave together the workings of mind, body, and spirit.

Neff and Germer's yin-yang of self-compassion as self-care, described in the introduction to this book, presents a similar dichotomy.[85] The yin elements that comfort, soothe, and validate can be realized through the activities that comprise part I of this book, as we move deeply into the music to investigate our feelings. The yang elements protect you, provide for your needs, and enhance motivation that stems from love, not fear. These tend to be more active ways of preserving your identity and expressing yourself. You protect yourself when you pause during a busy day to listen to music on one of your playlists, or when you incorporate music listening or active music-making into your daily routine. You are meeting your needs when you utilize music-based techniques to address concerns, change your mood, or cope with difficulties. You boost your motivation, when you are able to take action through creating and sharing music that advocates for issues that you feel strongly about.

Emily used music as a coping mechanism when she wrote a song that expressed her distress during the isolation of the pandemic. "I Got You" is a musical embrace that is meant to hold everyone around the world who is experiencing similar emotions.

Listen to Emily's music, "I Got You" here. Here are her lyrics.

61

"I Got You" by Emily

Today I sat down on the grass
And I thought about where we all are now
I really tried to run away
From this built-up rage
I guess I lost today

Chorus:

We play all the games, we share all the laughs
We ride this wave and pray we don't crash
At the end of the day
I hope you're safe
I hope you're safe

All I want to say is, if you've had a long hard day
I'm standing right there with you too
All I want to do is hold on tight to you and tell you
My friend, I've got you
My friend, I've got you

Last night, I had a vivid dream
We all were dancing in sweet harmony
Arms wrapped around each other tight
Like we only had one last night of our lives

(Chorus)

Emily explains:

> There is comfort in going through hard times knowing you aren't the only one going through it. I think this applies to anything in life. The emotions we feel as humans are universal, and at some point or another, we can relate to each other. Because of this, we get to show up for others, and others get to show up for us. Letting yourself receive support when you are struggling is brave, and it is something we have been taught to try and avoid. How many of us say "I'm fine," when we are really breaking inside? How many of us feel weak when asking for support? I know I have felt this way a lot in my life, and I continue to try and let go of those stories.
>
> When people listen to this song, I want them to feel relief knowing that we are all in this together. I want people to feel inspired to show up for others and allow others to show up for them. I want to shatter the beliefs that needing support makes you weak. I want people to know that it is okay to feel a lot and that you don't need to feel it all alone.

Listen to Emily's description.

62

Emily's optimism bestows an uplifting gift upon us with her music, and her positivity serves to improve her own sense of wellness. When we focus on others and empathize with their plights, we acknowledge that we are not alone and engage actively in the yang of self-compassion. Emily is letting go and allowing us to peek inside her psyche to access the resources that we need to prevail.

When Tania lost her father, she didn't know how to handle her grief, but she turned to music for a vocabulary of expression. Tania speaks about her musical composition "Respiro" ("Breathe"), and recalls how she coped by using her creativity.

63

Listen to Tania's music. Her lyrics are in Spanish, shown with English translation.

"Respiro" ("Breathe") by Tania

Cuando ya no puedas más, sueña	When you can't take it anymore, dream
Pero no te duermas más, sueña	But don't fall asleep but, dream
Cuando ya no puedas, ama	When you can't take it anymore, love
No con sexo nada más, ama	Not with sex, but just love
Cuando ya no puedas más, canta	When you can't take it anymore, sing
No una nota nada más, canta	Not just a simple note, but sing
Cuando ya no puedas más, ríe	When you can't take it anymore, laugh
No una mueca nada más, ríe	Not just a grin, but laugh
Que cuando yo no puedo más, escribo	When I can't take it anymore, I write
Digo sueño, amo, canto, yo río	I dream, I love, I sing, I laugh
Miro a la muerte y vivo	I look at death and live
Miro a la vida y respiro	I look at life and breathe
Cuando ya no puedas más, baila	When you can't take it anymore, dance
Siente tu debilidad, baila	Feel your weakness, dance
Cuando cueste el avanzar, anda	When it gets hard to move forward, just walk
Sin prisa nada más, anda	No hurry, just walk
Cuando ya no puedas más, suelta	When you can't take it any more, let go
Perdona todo mal, vuelta	Forgive it all, let it go
Y en la larga oscuridad, brilla	And in the long darkness, shine
Sonríele a la vida, brilla	Smile at life, shine
Que cuando yo no puedo más escribo	When I can't take it any more, I dance
Digo bailo, vuelo, canto, yo brillo	I dream, I love, I sing, I laugh.
Miro a la muerte y vivo	I look at death and live
Miro a la vida y respiro	I look at life and breathe

Tania explains her process:

> I obsessively sang and composed, and I got myself into dancing full-time in order to process, help me digest, and express this big change that was happening in my life. Apart from music, Buddhism also helped me get through this. I have always been connected with the Buddhist philosophy, and together with music, it taught me presence, and

reminded me about gratitude. It taught me how to connect with my truth and how to accept death as part of life. But it was mainly music that helped me release every single part of the pain.

I knew music was the only thing that could help me travel the beginning of this new life. I did not think about it. It was an automatic response as music is intrinsic in me, and I have always used music to connect with this truth. Music is my safe space, and I feel so fortunate and blessed to feel music so profoundly....

I believe this song is a reminder of how blessed we are because we are alive, a powerful reminder to simply breathe and stay present. I always send this song to someone I know who might be grieving and feels the need for support through a very hard process. I believe listening to this message can help them reconnect with the simple things in life, those that we all have access to in order to make us feel better. I personally always get back to this song when I feel hopeless, when I feel life gets really tough. I play it, and I am reminded of how I got through the toughest time in my life, just reconnecting with all these simple things that make me smile and give me peace. We all grieve differently and have different preferences in what makes us happy, and that is okay. But what I believe is truly important is to know and connect to whatever it is we feel that gives us that peace of mind and soul, to what makes us smile, and hang on to that whenever is needed. Luckily, music is one of those things and the best thing is that it is accessible to every human being. Fortunately, we all have access to it and can all connect with music in very special and unique ways.

Listen to Tania's story.

64

Tania teaches us how music strikes a chord when we express our strongest values and deepest feelings through our music. She emphasizes the glory of being alive in her music and inspires us to find the music in our lives and bring life to music. When she speaks of these blessings, she shows us how her music is also a gratitude practice that provides a balm for the pain of grief.

EXPRESSING GRATITUDE

Gratitude has been described as the best of life's virtues, bringing attention to the benefits of living and appreciation of others and the natural world. When we choose to bring awareness to reflect on what we are grateful for, we reap all sorts of benefits, including enhanced wellbeing and happiness.[86] When we express gratitude as a consistent practice, we gain improvements in psychological and physical health, although these effects are somewhat variable.[87] From gratitude journals to affirmative prayers, gratitude can be communicated in many ways. However, when we give thanks in the form of lyrics, the message can get stuck in our heads, and the accompanying music strengthens the emotional impact.

GRATITUDE AND LOVE

Bella takes a rather mundane subject, drinking coffee on Sunday mornings, as the inspiration for a love song.

Listen to Bella's song, "Coffee." Here are her lyrics.

65

"Coffee" by Bella

Sunday mornings with you feel like minutes
Sunday nights are the same
So before we both finish our coffee
Allow me to sing my praise

Lonely hearts just like mine are for taking
If you'll have me, that is
I can picture us both at home baking
Alongside all three of our kids

   Chorus:

   You know how to pull all the right strings
   And you know my favorite things
   Like how to make my coffee with just enough cream
   Loving with you is a dream

I get lonely when you're not around me
Even if you're next door
You fill my life with all kinds of sunshine
It's something I love and adore

(Chorus)

And hopefully one day I'll sing this song
And you'll know all the words and you'll sing along
'Cause I think I know you pretty well too
Allow me to prove that I do

Chorus:

I know all of your favorite things
And I know that you're shy when you sing
I know you like your coffee with sugar and cream
Loving with you is a dream (repeated)

Bella describes her song:

When writing this song, I was overcome with feelings of love and gratitude for this person whom I had chosen to share my time and love with. The lyrics seemed to write themselves. I knew going into the writing process that I wanted it to be a waltz, as this type of song feels so loving. The rest of the song came naturally, as if my thoughts had manifested into the music.

I began with my chord progression, playing it over and over, allowing the words to fall into place. I felt the creative flow as I was writing, unable to shift my thoughts to anything else. This sense of flow, for me, feels like I'm in a bubble of sorts, where the only things that exist are myself, my music, and my intentions. I think that viewing the creative process as something that encapsulates you can be useful to a lot of songwriters, as too often we are concerned with how other people will view our music. To step outside of this criticism and allow yourself to enter this "bubble," you are allowing yourself to exist wholly with yourself and your music.

When I played this recording for myself, I was filled again with all of the love and light I felt when I wrote this song. I felt lighter somehow, and the world felt kinder. I thought of my boyfriend and his smile when I first played this song for him, or the times since when we've sung the chorus together. This song, to me, feels like what love sounds like.

Listen to Bella's narrative.

66

CODA

When we acknowledge and explore our pain and struggles by engaging in mindful reflection, we are practicing radical compassion. Tara Brach provides a recipe through the acronym of RAIN:

R: Recognize and acknowledge what is happening inside of us.

A: Allow whatever arises to bubble up over time before we react to it.

I: Investigate with tender curiosity.

N: Nurture and care for yourself and others.[88]

I like to add an E: Extract meaning and Express through music.

CHAPTER 7

See the Images

🔊
Listen to my musical intention with the hang drum, and my accompanying description.

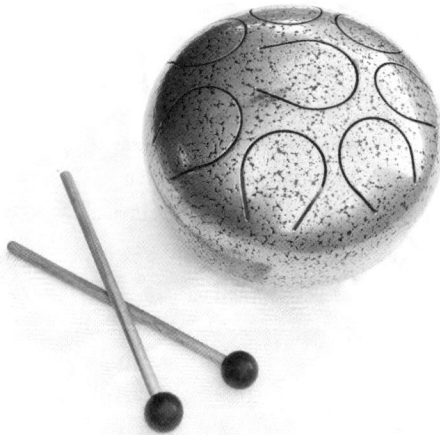

Hang Drum. Photo by Alan Teperow

I greet my neighbor, Claire, on her eighty-fifth birthday. I kiss her tissue-paper cheek and notice the mirror in her eyes. The reflection is not of my face, but my grandmother's, who has been gone for thirty years. I hear the whoosh and crackle of an old recording from inside Claire's house. The music is "Rozhinkes mit Mandlen" ("Raisins and Almonds"), my grandmother's favorite Yiddish song.

Suddenly, I am four years old and listening to my grandmother singing.

"Shluff, mein kindele, shluff," she sings. "Sleep, my little one, sleep."

I remember my grandmother telling me everything she remembers about the song:

> My mother sang this to me when we lived in Russia. Then, when I was your age, we came to America and here we were at Ellis Island, and those days, they're all a blank. But, my mother, she sang to me, and I remember every word—every word. I must have closed my eyes the whole time we were there. That way, I wouldn't have to be there at all. I could close my eyes and be back home in Russia, eating raisins and almonds with my mother. Come, mein kindele, come, we will eat some raisins and almonds, and you will learn to sing.

My heart seems to be pumping out this dialogue in time with the music. I am gazing at Claire, but my grandmother is here. This music is magic. It has sent me back to a time more than sixty years ago, and I see my grandmother vividly, smell her sweet and sour perfume, taste the chicken baking, and feel every shrivel in the raisins we are eating.

Actually, it's just the limbic system. This primitive center of our brains, the part that even reptiles have, is responsible for this time travel. The music is a powerful stimulus, triggering the hippocampus, amygdala, hypothalamus, and thalamus, the four nuggets of the limbic system. They go wild with electrical impulses.

The hippocampus has stored our long-term memories for a lifetime, and now here they are, in our consciousness, in our imaginations, feeling very real and present. That's the amygdala's doing. Coincidentally, the amygdala is almond-shaped, and its function is to link our experience directly to emotion, without the necessity of accessing the frontal cortex, the thinking part of our brains. The emotional connection to the music is immediate. We don't need to identify the piece by name or remember where we heard it. We are moved, often deeply, listening to a song that is beautiful to our ears.

The hypothalamus may be giving us goose bumps or chills, raising our blood pressure, or speeding up our heartbeats. It tells the body to react to what it is hearing. The thalamus is the relay station that conducts all this business and it does so in a heartbeat or less. Like a stationmaster, it creates the proper tracks and pathways for brain-body connections to be made. It is this miracle of circuitry that allows everyone who can hear music to respond to it, regardless of intellectual or physical capacity. All this is happening deep inside the brain's limbic system.

Back in Claire's home, I am exhilarated to have had this lovely visit with my grandmother. On the way home, I think about my friend Barbara, who lost her husband Bob two years ago.

The following week, I find myself in Barbara's attic. She and I are looking through boxes and boxes of Bob's record collection. There is opera, classical music, Frank Sinatra, Frankie Valli, Bing Crosby, and other men whom Barbara is now swooning over. We fill our arms with one of each genre and meet downstairs at the stereo.

Barbara plays "Come Fly with Me," crooned by Frank Sinatra, and soon, we are rushing about to find tissues to sop up our sorrow. Or, is it sorrow? In the next moment, we are laughing, as Barbara recounts Bob's attempts to imitate the romantic vibrato of the famous singer. We are chatting and reminiscing, crying and giggling, and gasping through our feelings of loss and love.

"I feel better than I have since I lost Bob," Barbara says. "It's like he's right here with us again."

So Barbara feels it, too—the sense that with the music comes a presence so real and true. We know he is not here, but something of his essence is. His music has brought the best of Bob right here in this room, visiting with us.

We would like to understand this phenomenon—the way the music associated with someone connects us so strongly, so viscerally. But, remember that music crosscuts the thinking brain and awakens so many other brain regions. Perhaps it is not as important to explain it than to "know" what it does for us.

The images that Barbara and I saw in our minds' eyes were visceral and vivid. My memory evoked a full sensory experience with my grandmother at the center. Barbara keenly felt Bob's presence and love. When we listen to music, it enters our ears without any coaxing. It penetrates our psyches without following any instructions. It goes to the heart without our pondering whether or not we want to be affected by it. We cannot will this music to move us. Its associations kick us right in the limbic system and we react reflexively.

COMING HOME

Throughout the pandemic, Minxue (Mint) was studying in the United States and unable to travel to see her family in China. As a pianist, Mint found a familiar place at the instrument, and the music she created brought her right back into her beloved home. Composing, performing, and listening transported her there and helped her cope with her homesickness and sense of isolation.

Listen to Mint's music, "Missing Home."

69

Mint explains her process:

Before I started to play, I asked myself, "What does home mean to me?" "What are some of my favorite memories from home?" and "What are some of the sounds and rhythms that evoke a sense of familiarity and comfort?" It was a process fulfilled with reflection and introspection at the beginning, and then, after I started to play, I was able to enter a state of flow. This is a state of mind where creativity comes easily and naturally, and time seems to fly by. It is a feeling of being fully immersed in the present moment and the task at hand. I found that this state of flow was particularly important when creating self-soothing music, as it allowed me to channel my emotions and experiences into the playing. When I play, I listen to the piano, just like someone sitting back and listening to a CD, except I can manipulate the sound at will. I focus on how I feel emotionally, and my past experiences flow through and echo that emotion. The sound I play arouses and inspires my emotions, while guiding me to continue playing.

The music I played creates a sense of calm and comfort within me. It reminds me of the familiar sounds and rhythms of home, and brings to mind memories of loved ones and past experiences. The music has a grounding effect, helping to anchor me in the present moment and easing my feelings of homesickness. When I listen back to the music I played, I observe a sense of relaxation in my mind and body. My breathing becomes slower and more controlled, and my muscles relax. I feel a sense of peace and contentment, and my worries and anxieties fade away. It is a powerful reminder that music has the ability to soothe and heal, even in the midst of difficult and challenging times.

Listen to Mint's entire story.

At the piano, Mint conjures up the sounds of home, and then paints a picture of her memories through the musical elements that comprise her emotional vocabulary. This is music of her memories; yet, it engulfs her in the present and brings her the comfort of home in the moment.

Bella remembers her late older brother, and a plaintive tribute rises out of her reminiscence. She is singing to him, about him, and for him, and we listeners catch a glimpse of the two of them together at home.

Listen to Bella's song, "Home." Here are her lyrics.

"Home" (Aziz's Song) by Bella

I don't know if you'd remember
All the times I cried alone in my room
When you'd come through my door
And sing me songs that made me feel at home
There were times when I felt like
I couldn't do anything worthy at all
But you always proved me wrong
With songs of love and smiles that felt like home
And I will never move on
I'll never write songs that sound
Half as good as you did
But still I'll try to write
Songs that remind me of you
And of home

Bella tells us about her process:

I wrote this song on the three-year anniversary of my older brother's death. I had just gotten home from school and was so overcome with emotions. I had been crying the whole day, and I knew that music would be a healing power for me. So, I took out my guitar and just started playing. The entire time I was writing, I thought about all of the memories I have with my brother. I sing about the times he has comforted me and made me smile, and I thought of the love he had for our family.

Usually when I write, I already have a melody or chord progression in mind that I want to use. For this song, however, I simply let the music manifest through my guitar and my voice. I started playing what felt natural and then began humming a melody that came to mind. After this, I began singing what felt right to the melody I had just created.

For the most part, the lyrics came pretty naturally to me, but I did have to step back and focus on good memories a few times, as my anger was starting to manifest into the lyrics, and that was not what I wanted to be the intention behind the song. I asked myself what the best intention would be for the song and how the lyrics could be used to show that intention. I then wrote the song as if I were speaking to him, singing about the things I remembered most and how I will do my best to honor his memory.

During this process, I felt like the music truly shaped how I handled my emotions. I went from crying and having trouble breathing to being calm and at peace, knowing that the love I have for my brother can never be diminished. This song helped me to change my thoughts from angry at his death to gratitude for his life....

When people listen to this song, I hope that they are able to feel the love I put into the words. I hope they feel the calming embrace that I believe the guitar gives. Most of all, however, I hope they too can take comfort in knowing that such strong memories can be turned into something beautiful, something you can be proud of. I hope this song can calm those in distress or help people reflect on loved ones they might be missing.

Listen to Bella's narrative and her loving story about Aziz.

72

Mint and Bella are time travelers. In creating their music, they are not only preserving special memories, but also reliving them, and communicating the essence of these times to us as listeners. Music offers us this gift of time. But, unfortunately, not everyone is capable of accessing memories so easily.

MEMORIES IN DISORDER

There are a number of neurological conditions that get in the way of memory retrieval and affect how we function and think. Dementia is a set of symptoms whereby short-term memory, reasoning, problem-solving, and thinking are compromised. Alzheimer's disease is a chief culprit, but there are other serious illnesses, like vascular dementia and Parkinson's disease that can cause these cognitive challenges, and the effects may be irreversible. Even some benign problems, like infections and lack of sleep, may result in temporary dementia.[89] Yet there is a way to help people with dementia focus their attention and retrieve memories associated with strong emotions and meaningful times.

Remarkably, memories of music seem to be highly preserved, even in some people who have advanced illness and severe dementia. Jörn-Henrik Jacobsen and colleagues found that the region of interest in the brain involved in musical memories is also one of the areas least affected by the neurological deterioration brought on by Alzheimer's disease.[90] Anecdotal evidence of music's ability to awaken individuals with serious cognitive problems include people who have not spoken but can sing along to a well-known song, and those who fail to recognize a loved one but play an entire piece on piano.

Fran leads activities in an assisted living facility with a memory care unit. Because of Fran's love of music, she infuses music into much of the day. She offers an example of someone whose musical memories remain intact.

> In the memory care unit, the effects of neurological conditions, such as Alzheimer's disease, are poignantly observable. I am often overwhelmed with emotion, witnessing the profound calming effect of music on residents with advanced memory loss. Even if they are aggressive, agitated, distracted, confused, uncommunicative, or unresponsive to human efforts, they respond to music. Music is, indeed, the great communicator, the great healer!
>
> One of the most touching examples of music's calming effect occurred with a resident in her early sixties who has early-onset Alzheimer's disease. Let's call her Mary. She is nonverbal and is a human perpetual motion machine. She

paces the corridors day and night, cannot sit for more than a few minutes, and is unable to participate in any of our group activities.

I asked a relative what kind of music Mary enjoyed and learned that she once played the violin and loved classical music. So, one day, during a quiet period, I invited them to the activity room and selected a video of the Tchaikovsky violin concerto.

The minute Mary looked up at the big-screen TV and heard the music, her usual rigid expression softened. She sat down (which was a miracle in itself!), mesmerized by the music and colorful closeups of the violinist, orchestra, and the audience. It was the only time I had seen her still. It was as though a magical force field beamed down from the screen to envelop and soothe her.

She then began commenting (in words unintelligible to us) on the performance. Each time she heard a difficult passage, she would nod her head "yes," as though appreciating the performer's skills. It was evident she could assess at some mysterious level the quality of the music. She sat perfectly still for about fifteen minutes, and her relative was amazed. Music does, indeed, do what medicine cannot do.

Listen to Fran's experience with Mary.

73

You can imagine the response of Mary's relative when she witnesses Mary's recognition of the violin performance. Unfortunately, there are no medicines to counteract the decline of neurological activity due to Alzheimer's disease, but music opens a channel to access memories and abilities that were seemingly lost. For all of us, regardless of our ability to think, reason, and remember, music can be a fountain of youth. When we listen to the music we enjoyed many years previously, we can often recall the tune and lyrics quite reliably. We are right back in that moment, savoring the felt sense of it all, and perhaps feeling young again.

WORLDS OF IMAGINATION

Those images that enter our minds through our memories can transform our emotions and our behavior. They can be beautifully translated into musical compositions that seem to capture the core meaning of our life experiences. They can bring us to another time or place. For Nomuki, her imagination conjures up a love story expressed through her musical composition.

74 Listen to Nomuki's music, "Summer Dream." You can also follow the lyrics.

"Summer Dream" by Nomuki

Summer has gone
I left my mind there
You'll never know how it feels—cruel again
No, I still remember your eyes
It was pure as the blue sun
I feel I have it all
"Lose your mind, then love again"
You only know it sounds just cruel again
No, I still remember your face
It was pure as the poems she wrote
I have nothing now

Chorus:

Your blue eyes
I think I am drowning again
Our whole tale
They'll never ever find it
But you've never left me alone
When I am laying on the ground
"We'll still remember," you said
Because of our summer dream (tea)! [Repeats]

He tried to be cool
But you never tried
I might see how you smile again
Now you know how it hurts me
More than anything else, and you'll remember

(Chorus)

You saw me there and smiled at me
Time just stops when you're with her
I could not talk for some months
You're singin' there like a ghost

You kissed my head held my hand
It's like a dream that someone had
But I still care about you now
You might see I love you

(Chorus)

Will you remember me
after all this time, my dear?

Nomuki describes her songwriting process:

> The song I wrote, "Summer Tea" (later, called "Summer Dream"), came to my mind three years ago. The song is based on a story I experienced. I used to go to my cottage house during the summer time, and I noticed everything while I was in the car. The people with many cars, their words, the trees, flowers, and our dreams all guided me to somewhere beautiful, which ended up like this beautiful story. My imagination went so wild at that time, and I started to think of other people's feelings and how they were dealing with those experiences differently.
>
> For this song, it is all about when you are in love with someone who is never meant to be. First and foremost, it seems a sad and tragic story—that you are falling in love with a person who is not destined to love you. But you started to notice something is changing inside you, and that power made you feel alive, and you forgave yourself for being in love, and accepted that those things had happened to you. This is a song about gratitude and details how that person you love tried to stand by your side and you always being the same person, no matter what is going on in your life. Everything happens for a reason. The things we should be grateful for in the process that makes us feel alive, even if it is hard to imagine or live through. At the end, the person you love came back to you in your imagination, and you knew that this ending was meant for you.

Listen to Nomuki's narrative.

75

Nomuki's story and soundtrack are inspired by nature's display in a place she loves. June's forest is also a sacrosanct place within the natural universe.

76

Listen to June's music, "Autumn Woods."

June describes the scene and how you can center yourself with her music.

> Sit crossed legged with raised palms, and close your eyes. In the intro of the music, with the nature sounds and harp, "awaken" to the forest around you. Sense the crisp air and smell of wet dirt, connected to the sky and the earth and drawing energy from them. You can picture what your personal woodland looks like. Then stop in the center of your woods and begin to dance with the music. Light glows from within you, and your movements help to direct it so that it swirls around you into a sphere of glowing energy. It fluctuates with the rises and falls of the music. At the apex of this music, release this energy, sending out light and blessings for you and the area around you. Rest during the final musical coda.

> I hope that this music helps you create a magical circle of peaceful energy for meditation, especially when you feel unbalanced or need to ground yourself.

Listen to June's description.

77

June's Autumn Woods. Photo by June Westfield

CREATING RITUALS

June designed a ritual to ground ourselves in nature. She stopped to notice and honor the moment, and created a practice of reverence to the trees in the rain. Her music celebrates this common occurrence, gives it special meaning, and allows us to savor the scene and the senses that are aroused in its midst.

Rituals generally commemorate a special time of life, transition, or milestone, and can create a sacred space in an otherwise ordinary place. When we do this, we take time to curtail routine, honor a person, respect a time, acknowledge a change, or celebrate an event. The purpose may also be to explore the meaning of this moment, and create a memorable time around it.

A ritual is a ceremony in which there are a series of actions that occur in a specific order in a precise place. Many rituals are associated with religious services, but they do not necessarily have to be religious. Symbolic objects and spiritual language are often involved, but simple habits can also qualify. We may have a morning ritual that includes washing, brushing teeth, and having coffee. We may have an evening ritual of eating dinner and calling loved ones to catch up on the day's activities.

While marriages and graduations almost always include rituals, consider a transitional moment that does not traditionally have a ready-made convention. You can craft a celebration and add some music to make it extra special. Do you or does someone you know have a new home, job offer, an "A" on an exam, or a task well-done? Rituals may help people through a difficult phase of life. Have you or has someone you know just experienced a breakup, divorce, relocation, or challenging diagnosis? This is another chance to provide a ritual acknowledging that this is hard, but it reminds us that this is only a temporary state. A ritual to recognize the adversity and its associated emotions, while emphasizing the support, love, and other factors to help the person through the struggle, can reframe even the most complicated obstacles.

Is there an opportunity for a ritual in your world? Here are some tips:

1. **Offer an intention.** Decide upon the purpose of your ritual. Who should be involved, and where will it take place? How can you bring a sense of peace and gratitude to this opportunity?

To begin the ritual, identify music that has personal meaning to you or the person you are honoring. You might consider "Turn! Turn! Turn!" by the Byrds, a song that speaks to the seasons of life and a "time to every purpose." "Stand by Me" by Ben E. King is about being there for someone always, no matter what happens. There are many songs about transitions, hope, gratitude, and peace that can set the stage and mood.

2. **Create a theme song.** Select or compose a song that can be sung, played, or chanted to celebrate this significant moment or offer a sense of acceptance of a difficult situation. Consider songs that imbue the listener with hope, e.g., "We Are the Champions," "You're the Best," "I Feel Good," "It's a Beautiful Day," or "With a Little Help from My Friends." Add movement and dance to energize the mood, and embody the intention of the ritual.

3. **Send blessings.** What would provide just what you (or other person) might need or desire? Articulate this in a chant or jingle, e.g., "May you be surrounded by love," "May you have success after success."

4. **Collect special objects.** Are there symbols of love or peace that are meaningful to you or others who are important to you, e.g., greeting cards, photographs, mementos, magazine pictures, affirmations, books, etc.? Include these and other objects, like a pebble or flower that can symbolize something you wish to convey, e.g., a rock for the strength required through this transition, a flower to show the growth that you have (or this person has) shown through the experience. This may provide another opportunity for a song or chant to describe their importance. You can also write a simple song about leaving something behind and taking in something new, e.g., "I breathe out my frustration, and I take in a deep breath," or "I want to let go of fear and bring in optimism."

5. **Find a fitting finale.** How can you bring closure to your ritual? What will be an appropriate send-off? Is there a musical gift for you or the person involved? Perhaps there is an optimistic song that speaks to the future, addresses the meaning of the ritual, or engages everyone present in celebration of the person.

6. **End with silence.** It is always nice to provide space for processing the ritual. Silence offers this opportunity without judgment.

Journal about this experience or debrief with participants, as you wish. This ritual will create new memories to associate with this time in your life.

OUR VAST IMAGINATIONS

When you listen to music with your eyes closed, do you see pictures in your imagination or mind's eye? Some people experience vivid images when they listen to music. They might see the place where they last heard this music. They can visualize the people who were with them when they heard that music. They may imagine a familiar, comforting location or a fantastical place that doesn't actually exist. They might automatically return to a memory associated with this music.

If you are listening to music that is meaningful to you, you may identify many different sensations and pictures in your mind. You may notice changes in your breathing and physiology, emotions, thoughts, connections, inspirations, memories, meaning, intuition, or spiritual insight. Enjoy these rich responses in your whole body, and marinate in them. You are learning how your mind, body, and spirit are integrating through meaningful musical experiences and rituals.

GUIDED IMAGERY AND MUSIC

Music therapists use music and the sort of imagery that we have been exploring to help others. A popular, evidence-based methodology is the Bonny Method of Guided Imagery and Music (BM-GIM). Helen Lindquist Bonny developed this special set of techniques to allow music listeners to explore self-understanding. Practitioners complete specialized training in order to support and safely guide the experience through:

1. preliminary conversation to establish rapport and purpose

2. induction, as a person listens to the facilitator's cues to relax

3. music listening (twenty to forty minutes of selected classical pieces), while the listener reports on imagery and thoughts that come to mind

4. processing and reflecting on the music and imagery experience[91]

Music is a remarkable stimulus for relaxation, self-exploration, and personal insights. The images and memories that are evoked by the music may be symbolic of issues that carry profound or spiritual meaning. A qualified facilitator can masterfully use the music as a creative catalyst to access a deeper state of consciousness, and to enable the listener to delve into the metaphors and experiences that potentially bring personal growth and greater self-understanding. Because the experience can evoke some powerful reactions, I strongly recommend that you listen to music with a friend or someone you trust, and share your experiences. This support is an important part of processing the music, and may open you to more creative interpretations. You might be surprised at what transpires.

TAKE A WALK IN YOUR MIND'S EYE

Dr. Maria Hernandez is a music therapist at a cancer center. Her piano improvisation is intended to take people far away from the chemotherapy infusion unit and have them imagine taking a walk in a beautiful place with a trusted companion. As you listen to Maria's music and explore, you can go anywhere and take anyone with you. But you need not plan ahead or move a muscle. You can just let the music take you there.

Listen to Maria's music (which she guides us through), "We Never Walk Alone."

78

Maria describes her creation.

> This improvisation is one that comes about really in the moment, when I am in a room with a patient or with the staff sometimes in the infusion unit, and I just want to calm the environment. I just place my fingers on the keyboard and just really not think a lot about what I'm going to play, but allow how I feel to come through my playing, if that makes sense. It's almost as if you are creating a dialogue in the moment without really knowing where it's going or how it's going to end, but trusting that while we're in the moment and playing, that we're able to convey that expression and feeling of calm and peace and serenity. When I'm next to my patient, I try to assess how they are in the moment, think about the type of melody that they may want or need to listen to in the moment, and then improvise with that

melody or the chords, and in a sense, kind of take them on a journey with me, as I am too, on the journey with my improvisation. It helps bring good memories, it helps calm the body and the mind, and it allows a person to really find a place of peace during a time of much difficulty.

Listen to Maria's explanation of how she improvises at the piano.

Whether it elicits vivid imagery, sparks memories, or simply induces a change in how you feel, music moves you along in real time with its changing motifs and motives. Where would you like to go and who would you bring along?

IMAGINING YOUR FUTURE

The images in our minds, whether uprooted by memory, physical space, personal connections, or a vision of the future, nourish our imaginations. "Imagination is more important than knowledge. Knowledge is limited. Imagination encircles the world." So said Albert Einstein in 1929, in an interview with *The Saturday Evening Post*.[92] As music cultivates imagination, let it be our guide to travel worlds inside and out, past, present, and future.

CHAPTER 8

See the Other

80,81

Watch this video (or listen to the audio) of a virtual ensemble, "Music is…" and listen to my accompanying description.

David was referred to music therapy by his psychiatrist because he was not responding to other treatments. He had displayed serious depression for much of his life, and there didn't seem to be a medication or therapy that had any significant impact on his overall sadness, pessimism, irritability, and malaise. At our first meeting, David sat across from me with a tension that made it seem as though his wrists and ankles were shackled to the chair. I told David that I liked to initiate our sessions with music, and so, began to improvise on my Native American flute, as I customarily did. He softened into the chair and lifted his eyebrows.

"I can't remember when I felt so good," he said. "You know, for a moment, I felt like I was in the forest, where I used to go as a child, where I could be alone. And just now, I felt the breeze and smelled the wildflowers. I was so glad to be back where I was as a boy. Life was so much simpler then."

"So you found that little boy inside you?" I asked.

He arched back and I thought the chair would topple. His arms dangled while his eyes searched the ceiling for an answer.

"Uh huh. I was pretty much a loner, then. I didn't like people, didn't know what to do with them, didn't know how to make contact, make friends. But, you know what? The forest settled me. I found the birds and bugs there. They were kinder to me than people. Rocks were unbreakable, and stayed where I left them."

"Okay," I said. "Let's go back to that forest, Mr. Bartlett. Let's feel what it's like to be carefree. What shall I play for you?"

He pointed to my dulcimer, and I nested it in my arms.

"Can you play 'Tis a Gift to Be Simple'?"

That lovely Shaker melody was perfect for inducing a sunlit forest. I began strumming a major chord, and invited him to close his eyes and breathe with the music.

"Let the music surround you," I said, "and see where it takes you."

I sang the lyrics, and his lips moved with mine.

"So you know the words. Would you like to sing together?" I asked.

If he enjoyed singing, he would be able to bring music with him whenever he needed to change his mood. His hands conducted with determination as he sang all the words, perfectly in pitch, in a bounding, buzzing baritone.

"You have a magnificent sound."

"I know," he said, with unexpected pride.

Indeed, I had not anticipated such power and confidence. When he belted out, he was outgoing. He smiled as he sang, his eyes opened wide, and his cheeks turned pink. Deep, sustained notes spilled out of his eyes and nose, and his voice reverberated against every surface. It was my job to show him how he could maintain this animated persona through adversity. Over the next few weeks, David practiced breathing deeply and singing with gusto, filling his body with energy. He would learn how to show an array of emotions in a strong, active voice. When he began to feel down or nervous or uncomfortable, he would be able to replace these sensations with musical affirmations and a repertoire of favorite songs. We roleplayed scenarios that caused distress, together found a musical alternative to counteract the emotion, and had him play out his strategy on the spot.

I demonstrated a systematic desensitization procedure[93] in which music assuaged some of David's fears, and conditioned a relaxation response to some aversive situations. We wrote songs that showed optimism and hope. David imagined himself amongst people—meeting a friend at a movie, inviting a family member out, attending a concert—and he told those stories through his original songs. We probed the barriers that prevented him from reaching out to others, and he began developing creative techniques to embolden himself to try new things.

I knew we were on the right track, when of his own volition, David joined a choir.

A CHORUS LINE

I was excited for David, not just because this act was emblematic of reaching outside his insular world to engage in a group activity, or because singing in a choir is fun and a great way to meet people, but because making this choice is actually a healthy one for both mental and physical wellness. A large international investigation found that choristers appreciated six general benefits: social connection, cognitive stimulation, physical/physiological health (particularly respiratory health), mental health, enjoyment, and even a sense of transcendence.[94] While engaged in singing, participants in another study reported an expanded state of flow, as supported by decreased activity of adrenocorticotropic hormone (ACTH), a measure of arousal produced in response to stress.[95] Specific improvement in immune function (secretory immunoglobulin A or sigA) was found in choir participants,[96] and a study of singers who have cancer showed changes in a variety of hormones and immune function markers, including oxytocin, cytokines, cortisol, and β-endorphins.[97]

Before the pandemic, Chorus America estimated that there were 42.6 million individuals taking part in choruses in the U.S.[98] During the pandemic, there was even a drive to bring choir members together safely by having them sing in their cars, as documented in the film *The Drive to Sing*.[99] Chorus members in each vehicle used portable mics and tuned into the same radio frequency, while coordinators used mixers to combine the individual tracks. Obviously, singers are committed and creative! Now that COVID-19 restrictions have been repealed, people are lining up to sing in all sorts of vocal ensembles. Will you join them?[100]

GETTING TOGETHER

Why all this fuss about getting together? Very simply, research supports age-old philosophies that having a good life is determined by the quality of our human connections and meaningful relationships. In the book *The Good Life: Lessons from the World's Longest Scientific Study of Happiness*, Robert Waldinger and Marc Schulz describe the findings from the Harvard Study of Adult Development, a longitudinal investigation that began in 1938 and continues to follow 1,300 individuals today.[101] Amongst a complex network of factors affecting health and flourishing, connection and relationship emerged as the strongest by far.

Yet for some, reaching out to others and engaging in social relationships are awkward and challenging. If meeting others is difficult for you, music ensembles and classes provide structure and regularity for being with others. If you are not convinced that singing in a chorus is for you, there are as many benefits for instrumental ensembles and community music-making.[102] Consider the following:

- Joining a band, orchestra, or instrumental group
- Inviting others to play or sing with you in a duo, trio, or troupe of any number
- Attending/organizing a neighborhood or community concert or sing-along
- Taking a music or dance class
- Asking friends to meet up at a concert or musical/dance event
- Getting together for a music listening party, known by some as a "record pull." (Guests bring musical favorites, and you might find yourself singing and dancing along.)
- Hosting a gathering to celebrate life (or for no reason at all)
- Hiring local talent for a festivity
- Losing the earbuds and sharing your favorite music
- Replacing lonely, idle time with creative projects, practice, or rehearsal (and including others or sharing the results with them)

PLAYLISTS TO SHARE

One simple way to reach out to others is to share or create playlists for friends, family, and acquaintances. It's a great gift for anyone at any time, especially when you are at a loss for figuring out what you can do for someone in need. When a person you know is suffering, it may be difficult to know what to say or do. Sending them music that they might appreciate or helping them develop their own playlists is personal and generous. Of course, it is not necessary to have an occasion or a reason. An unexpected musical present can let someone know that you are thinking about them.

Gen is not a morning person, so she created this playlist to greet the morning. She offers it here as a source of inspiration for us. So let's get up and go!

GEN'S PLAYLIST

1. "Great I Am" (LaRue Howard)
2. "Bones" (Maren Morris)
3. "Sunrise" (Simply Red)
4. "Voyager" (Jean Leloup)
5. "Aime" (Bruno Pelletier)
6. "On Your Mind" (Kaskade)
7. "High Hope" (Pink Floyd)
8. "Jardim Do Universo" (Bettina Maureenji)
9. "Running Up That Hill" (Kate Bush)
10. "Freedom" (Wham!). This normally is the last one, or added in case of extreme need of a boost. :)

Gen explains her process in developing this playlist, developed initially to be a morning wake-up call:

> I embarked on this journey of testing various songs. Some were too up-tempo for the early hours, while others were too mellow. Yet, a select few resonated perfectly with me. In no particular order, these ten songs have become a staple of my morning playlist, helping me rise and gradually activate myself with confidence and determination.
>
> Indeed, certain songs have the power to transport me back to my youth when life seemed simpler and more carefree. There are also those that possess a spiritual essence, lifting my spirit, and inspiring a sense of elevation. This playlist is a delightful blend of diverse ingredients, each serving a unique purpose for my mind, body, and spirit. It's a harmonious combination that nourishes me in various ways. It liberates my mind from negative thoughts and makes me focus on what I have to do, that serves me best.
>
> I would love that this playlist serves as an inspiration for you to explore new songs, even in different languages or genres, perhaps, beyond your usual preferences. Encouraging an open-minded approach to music can lead to delightful surprises and enriching experiences that resonate deeply.

Listen to Gen's explanation.

Mark is a music therapist who works with children and families. His entrainment playlist brings the listener from lonely to connected. It is an example of how music can connect us, just by listening to an artist with whom we sense empathy.

MARK'S LONELY-TO-CONNECTED PLAYLIST

1. "Lonesome" (Kina Grannis)
2. "Palace" (Sam Smith)
3. "Distance" (Emily King)
4. "Light On" (Maggie Rogers)
5. "Count on Me" (Bruno Mars)
6. "Mr. Blue Sky" (Electric Light Orchestra)
7. "Another Night on Mars" (The Maine)
8. "Feel the Need" (Eryn Allen Kane)
9. "Parachute" (Ingrid Michaelson)
10. "I Wanna Dance with Somebody" (Whitney Houston)

Mark describes how he developed this collection of popular songs:

> Valued, seen, heard, belonging. There are many ways in which we as individuals seek connection in our daily lives. Having a community of others you feel bonded and close with can improve the quality of our lives, as we navigate the ever-changing paths our life journey takes us on. Throughout our lives, we may also experience loneliness as we navigate transitions and changes in our routine that create isolation and shifts in our social networks.
>
> Creating a mood playlist for these moments in life where loneliness may creep in can help us connect to our community even from afar and provide us with the connection we are seeking.

When I created this playlist, it was during a time in my life where I felt isolated as a result of COVID. My social networks were not physically available to me in the ways in which my mind sought them. I selected the pieces of music by reaching out to my community and asked them to send me their songs they access when they feel lonely, and then what songs they use to feel connected with others. From there, I organized the music into a spectrum from lonely to connected in a way that connected with me. Each song is from a different community member of mine that I feel connected to, and when I listen to this playlist, I can be reminded of the positive memories and connection I share with them. It is a way for me to keep my community close to me while I am alone. I end the playlist with "I Wanna Dance with Somebody" by Whitney Houston because this song for me creates a space for acknowledging the desire to be with my community, while also reminding me that I can create a sense of connection with myself through the music I listen to on my own. I often find myself dancing on my own to this song, whether it is in my home, or on my commute to work.

83 Listen to Mark's commentary.

When I discover a playlist like Mark's that attempts to match a mood using the iso principle and then entrain to a more desirable state, I allow myself to simply listen and feel what is going on in my mind, body, and spirit. When I find the music that resonates, there is a moment of connection that defies description. I sense a profound understanding from the artist's expression. I hope that you will take Mark's advice and allow others to help you create your own playlist for connection.

Gen and Mark are generous souls who speak to the solid link formed between them and the music that means a great deal to them. When we accept their suggestions, we receive more than their music.

MUSIC AS A SOURCE OF EMPATHY

The bonds described by Gen and Mark show "empathy," a form of "human mirroring." It is remarkable that when we see others show extreme feelings, our brains activate the same regions as theirs, so these connections are physical. So says Jamil Zaki, in *The War for Kindness: Building Empathy in a Fractured World.*[103] Zaki contends that empathy is a skill we can practice and hone, and in so doing, we more easily build resilience and grow in compassion and kindness. He reinforces the observation that artistic endeavors and telling our stories provide safe environments for expressing and exploring our emotions, while engendering empathy with others.

Indeed, when we share our music with others—this source of our memories, stories, and emotional journeys—our generosity goes beyond supporting our own personal wellness. We are disclosing an intimacy related to our internal life in the service of another's wellbeing. As a beneficiary, listening to this music tells us that we are not alone and that others understand how we feel and can see us for who we are. Actively and deeply listening to music can bond us in this way. Creating music and engaging others in music and dance has the ability to embody this connection even further.

MUSIC THAT HELPS

Caitlin is a music teacher and mother who often writes songs with her students and her young son, Jax. Since her husband's cancer diagnosis, she has been particularly concerned that Jax have an avenue to communicate and work out his feelings. She wrote this song with Jax to help him discover, name, act out, and understand different emotions.

Listen to Caitlin's and Jax's music, "How Are You Feeling?"

84

"How Are You Feeling?" by Caitlin and Jax

*I'm feeling **angry***
I'm not okay
*I want to shout out that **I'm having a bad day!!***
Stomp Stomp Stomp
Shout Shout Shout
*Stomp Shout let it out **"Grrrrr!"***
*I'm feeling **angry***

*I'm feeling **happy***
I'm feeling glad
*I want to jump for joy and hug my **Mom and Daddy***

Jump Jump Jump
Hug Hug Hug
*Jump Hug Cuddle Bug **"I love you Mommy"***
*I'm feeling **happy***

*I'm feeling **grumpy***
I'm feeling bad
*I think I want to cry because **I am so sad***
Cry Cry Cry
Pout Pout Pout
*Cry Pout Help me out **"Hmmm"***
*I'm feeling **grumpy hmmm!***

*I'm feeling **playful***
I'm feeling rad
*I want to play pretend and run around with **Daddy***
Shoot my webs
Strike a pose
*Everybody knows **"Go webs go!"***
*I'm feeling **playful***

Our feelings help us sort things out
Shout Hug Laugh or Pout
How are you feeling? (repeat with fade)

Caitlin explains the development of this song:

> I have used music as a means of "therapy" and to engage with my son from the very beginning of his wee life. We have recorded songs in the past, and we sing together every single day, whether we are improvising off each other or belting along to Disney soundtracks. It was a no-brainer that writing a song together to talk about how we are feeling these days might be useful and make a difference in the way Jax can process his emotions. I also wanted to stress the importance that it is totally okay to feel whatever he needs to feel—that we don't have to fix a "bad" feeling right away—that sometimes, we need to be angry, and we need to sit in that emotion together. In summary, I wanted this to be an accessible song for children who might be going through something in their lives where they are unable to process and express their feelings.
>
> We began the writing process by sitting down and having a conversation about how different situations make us feel different ways. I asked Jax a lot of questions in an effort to reflect and write his genuine responses and thoughts in the lyrics. I even would sing to him, *"I'm feeling..."* and he would just naturally respond with whatever he felt like in the moment—which really worked out for this particular song.

Ironically, when we started to record, Jax was feeling so angry, he just kept saying, "I can't record right now because I just can't now, Mommy!" I began to play the minor piano riff, and he started marching around, fists bunched into little balls at his side. I sang out, "I'm feeling...." and it was like he knew that was his cue: "*ANGRY!!! I'm NOT okay!*" It didn't work out perfectly like this for the entire recording process, and I did prompt him and ask him to say a line when necessary, but by the time we were finished, he had literally gone from screaming and refusing to try, to laughing, dancing, smiling, and having a really awesome time with Mommy. It was an emotional experience for me... and most certainly for him.

Since creating this piece, we have listened to it, as per Jax's request, multiple times every single day. To say he loves this song would be an understatement, and I must say, the feeling is mutual. He has little actions he acts out tied with every emotion in the piece. He sings along with the words and laughs uncontrollably when he hears his little voice over the speakers. This alone makes writing this song with him the biggest success I could have ever hoped for. There is no question I will do this with him again and again for as long as he will let me. The feelings I get from seeing his joy cannot be explained. I am amazed at how easily he picks up on each of the feelings talked about in our song, and the fact that he is acting these emotions out over the course of each verse shows me he truly understands what we are talking about. This is a huge triumph and goes to show our exercise of using music to process our emotions has really worked.

I know this is written for children for the purpose of understanding and expressing how one feels, but I think the same simple rules can apply to anyone of any age. Don't be afraid to write out exactly how you feel to create something that speaks *your* truth. It can be as simple or as complex as you choose to make it. If it gives you a sense of release, acceptance, and understanding of what is happening in your life, I think this tool can be a game changer in how you move forward, which brings me to my next point: I think it just goes to show how accessible, therapeutic, and fun songwriting can be. While songwriting and music production is something I would love to do and will study more in-depth, I am by no means a professional songwriter or producer, and neither is my three-year-old son. Literally *anyone* can do this. This is one of the reasons I wanted to bring Jax into this musical equation—to show you beautiful individuals that you can be any age and of any ability to make something special. You don't need to be Stevie Wonder or Paul Simon to reap the benefits and have success of creating your own music. It is personal. It is expressive. It is a part of who you are, coming to life through music and sound.

Listen to Caitlin's story about working through feelings with her "Songbird" music students, and her observations of the impact, as well as how her music affects her son.

85

Caitlin is not the only one who loves making music with children. Natalia is Nicky Mario's grandmother, and their relationship seems to be defined by their many musical interactions. Natalia tells us how they practice and sing together:

> Where do I begin to tell my story of Nicky Mario and the positive effects of music in his "Awesometistic LIFE?" Nicky Mario is now ten years of age and was diagnosed on the autism spectrum at age three years and nine months. As his Vóvó, (that's Portuguese for grandma), I have been with him daily over the last seven years, and very early on, I began witnessing the life-affirming aspects of singing music with Nicky. You name it, we sang it....
>
> I must confess that I have spent my whole life singing and performing OPM—that is, "other people's music," and the very idea of composing my very own tunes was somewhat of foreign nature to me. However, I wanted a lullaby for Nicky, and this text just fell out of me and fit into a little melody. Nicky fell asleep within seconds....
>
> Nicky Mario, born April 15, 2013, "tax day," as we taught him to say, is just the gem and light of Vóvó's Life. I feel that Nicky Mario is my gift from God/the Universe, a gift which comes as a blessed opportunity to unwrap one day at a time, one moment at a time, one note at a time. My statement unto the Universe is that music gives unto humanity the power and presence to live, love, lighten up, and laugh! And so it is.

"Sleep Well" by Natalia

Sleep well, my Nicky Mario
With all your angels by your side
The Light of God, the Love of God
The Peace of God are here to guide

There is no spot where God is not
I know the love inside the heart
The universe is on our side
A friendly place no need to hide.

One Source, One Love, One Life, One Boy
One power wisdom of the light
We've all been given inner sight
The laughter, love, and light and joy!

Listen to Natalia's story and performance of her lullaby.

86

MUSIC THROUGH THE LIFE CYCLE

Caitlin and Natalia have given us some wonderful models for engaging young people in music. For resources on other musical ideas you might use in your own life, you might like to consult activity books for families, like *All Together Singing in the Kitchen*[104] and Dan Zane's *House Party: A Family Roots Music Treasury.*[105]

We are all creative souls who play music and play with music throughout our lives. Your music is meant to be expressed and communicated, heard, and shared. There are, of course, endless possibilities for being with others in music, but here are just a few ideas for:

- Bonding with a baby, kangaroo style, by humming or singing in a deep, resonant voice with the infant on your chest (modeled expertly by my husband, Alan, with our grandchildren)

- Pacifying a baby or young child with your own lullaby or adapting one you know

- Personalizing a children's song or writing silly songs by replacing words with the child's name, interests, and having them fill in the blanks

- Composing songs to accompany daily activities, like brushing teeth or cleaning up

- Finding and crafting instruments from pots, pans, plates, and other household items that reverberate, and accompanying favorite music
- Chanting a call and response, where you make up the things you want to say, and asking your companion to repeat them back to you
- Moving and dancing to music or hosting a dance party to free up your spirits
- Making up some music on the spot and improvising with body percussion or instruments
- Finding new music to listen to and exploring the feelings that are elicited
- Playing music, engaging with it in some new way, and talking about whatever it brings up
- Listening to the favorite music of family members and friends of all ages, and discussing why they and you like it
- Teaching someone or learning a new song or instrument
- Reminiscing about cherished times and singing/dancing/playing/listening together
- Playing musical games, like "Name That Tune"
- Attending concerts, dances, and musical events together
- Creating playlists of loved ones' or friends' favorite music for them
- Recording your voice in a personal message along with music that carries a particular intention for someone in need (or as a surprise gift)
- Composing music and creating playlists for others
- Living the moment fully by celebrating with music that fits the mood and inviting others into the experience
- Reaching out to ask others to recommend music for you, then immersing yourself in their gifts, and sharing your response

MUSIC THERAPY

As a music therapist, Dr. Maria Hernandez' life mission is to help people heal through music. She tells the story of one of the many people in the cancer center who are the beneficiaries of her work there.

Ms. Suarez was a soft-spoken woman in her fifties and a mother of two who I had been working with during her chemotherapy. She was battling an aggressive cancer, and our work together was focused on music-assisted relaxation interventions focused on her breathing, and receptive listening to her music of preference. However, that day as I walked into her room, I observed a woman lying in bed, alone, and lost in her thoughts, while looking up to the ceiling as the chemo dripped into her IV....

The facial expression on my patients when they improvise on the pentatonic [five-note] scale for the first time is priceless. Introducing such an intervention to Ms. Suarez did not fail, and her facial expression of surprise was just as priceless. I instructed her to play the black keys, to trust the process and not to worry about the final product, and that I would be right at her side accompanying her with chords. I reminded her that as long as she stays within the black keys, no matter the order or how fast or slow she plays, it will sound beautiful. It was in playing her first notes that I took note of a change in her. The paradigm of a young woman lying alone in bed and in distress that I had walked into two weeks ago started to shift. She was now sitting up, with her hands on the keyboard, creating her melodies while I supported her with chords at her side, and where her motifs began to resound more assertively with each measure that passed.

Her giggles and smile at the end of her improvisation was an invitation of "Let's do this again." I suggested that we record it on GarageBand, so that she could have a recording of it. After recording her improvisation, I remember I had asked her how she would like to title it. I knew that encouraging my patient to give it a title would not only personalize her creative work but make it even more meaningful. However, it also allowed me to gain a deeper perspective on what this could mean for her. I am always intrigued on any thoughts that are elicited during this creative process and if it warrants processing. She was quick in giving it a title, when she looked at me and uttered the word: "Why?" And while I intuitively knew where this question was coming from, I asked her: "Why, why?" She looked at me and said, "Why me? Why cancer?"

It had been two weeks since Ms. Suarez had titled her improvisation "Why?" and it was in entering her room that day, that I realized that perhaps there was a way to help Ms. Suarez with music after all, especially when she immediately said that she had been sharing her improvisation recording with her family and mother. She stated with a smile, "I have been listening to it at home, it relaxes me, and I can hear myself asking the question "Why?" in my melody. Her calm while sharing how she finds meaning and peace in her improvisation was humbling. Her willingness to keep exploring her creativity with improvisation while the chemo continued to drip into her IV was reassuring.

When I find myself next to a patient in the infusion unit, I am instantly going down a list of chief complaints that the patient might be experiencing, while I implement that intervention with music in a way that the patient's needs are addressed and is yet still able to have a transformative experience. This is how healing occurs, in spite of diagnosis or prognosis. I knew that the music interventions I had implemented prior to Ms. Suarez' improvisation helped decrease pain perception and ameliorate her anxiety with its short-acting effect, but it was through her improvisation that I was put at ease. I learned with Ms. Suarez that sometimes our deepest sufferings are not one held in a list of chief complaints but sometimes held deep within us—unspoken many times in fear—until the music comes into our lives, giving us allowance to say out loud, "Why, why me?" which too can be healing and with a long-acting effect.

Listen to Maria's entire story here.

87

A MUSICAL GIFT

As the coda for this chapter and her gift, producer and composer Hélène wrote this music for us.

Listen to Hélène's music:

88

Hélène explains:

> I have always been a hypersensitive person. As many of my fellow artists, life can quickly become an overwhelming experience.
>
> Music, and sounds in general, have been my own therapy since I arrived on this planet. It became the most natural and powerful medicine for the mind and spirit, which also impacts the body. A way to connect to the spiritual/creative source, that guides me in everything I do. This source is luminous, full of love and compassion, and has a will to communicate it deeply....
>
> In my music, there is no lyrics, as a way to transcend cultures and a way to focus on what brings us together as earthlings. But lyrics are also an excellent way to help others. I think we all had these moments when we recognized our story in someone else's music. The identification is an excellent way to feel understood, and understanding is compassion, compassion is love, and love is a medicine. Let all that you do be done in love—and not only humans are helped, thanks to vibrations, but also every living being.

Listen and feel the love.

89

CHAPTER 9

See the Self

Listen to my musical intention, "Sounds of Home," and my accompanying description of this music.

For Reva, a child who was born with a condition much like cerebral palsy, music allows her to reveal what is inside. But because she cannot speak, because unlike me, she cannot communicate how music soothes or inspires or impassions, I cannot know all that music does for her. I can only guess.

In a language all her own, her favorite word pierces the air.

"Eemee!"

Reva's oversized forehead emerges over dark eyes, a perfect nose and delicate chin. I cannot decipher her stare. In the style of adolescent peers, her mahogany hair is tied back. Loose ringlets reveal a carefree nature at odds with her body. Her blouse is creaseless, patterned to match the full skirt that will never twirl. Well-made clothes fall at odd angles. The stiff brace encasing her torso keeps me from getting too close. As I search, looking for the keyhole to unlock Reva's world, she erupts again.

"Eemee!"

Hear me. Here! Me! Give me! What is she saying? What does she want? What does she feel?

She steps up her pace to greet me and tips into my body, as her mother lets go. Her fists unroll and clench my biceps—it is her hug—while she laughs deep from her center. She smiles openly, lots of tongue. Saliva drips, turning my collar a deep blue.

"Eemee!" she shouts, splattering me in a high soprano.

"Hello, Reva," I say.

Where are you today? I wonder.

At fourteen, Reva vocalizes when the radio is on, laughs with music, squeals to her father's piano-playing, and shoves him aside to make room on the bench. All her favorite toys are musical. I am hoping that music will help her communicate who she is, just as it has for me. When Reva's parents saw something inside her responding directly to music, they called me. I am Reva's music therapist.

"Eemee!" she exhales.

Help me get the yellow tambourine with the blue and red ribbons and the sunny cymbals. Help me sing a pretty song. Help me show you what I know. Help me be me.

"Reva, do you hear me?" I chant on two notes (a minor third) in a sing-song style.

She rocks back with a start, yelps, "Eemee," reaches with her wrist, jerks her chin left, then pulls a smile. Her body writhes. Neck hiccups, head topples, arms contort. Her back brace keeps her upright, keeps her steady.

"Hello, Reva, won't you come and play?" I sing.

I strike the tambourine. She convulses, guffaws. Her face shakes in laughter while her restrained body tries to sway to the swing-low rhythm.

"Hello, Reva, where are you in there?"

"Eemee!"

What do you say when you scream like that? Is it "Turn on that Pete Seeger music I love?" Is it "Smell those great cookies mom baked?" Is it "Let's see a Red Sox game?" Do you mean "What joy?" I think it can't be anything less. Your sound is too sharp, too full, too whole.

When I hear music, something happens to me. I want to scream like Reva, but I have been taught better. When I was a child, I learned to keep my feelings in. In check. Inside. In.

> Sit with your hands clasped. Your legs crossed. Behave. Don't make a fuss. Don't exclaim. Music is meant to be taken in, and don't let it out unless you have training.

How I envy that about you, Reva. Your feelings reverberate, intone, explode. Am I being true to you? Is it my joy for the music that I project onto you? No, perhaps it is the reverse.

You teach me what joy is. Unrestrained, unconcerned about the world's reaction, you speak in a language I have never learned. Your communication is raw; mine is reasoned, slower, dull, from the head. Your inflections range in pitch and intensity; my speech is limited within these dimensions. Your emotions are spoken out loud; mine are suppressed somewhere far beneath.

Reva, you speak truth; I find words that will please my listener. You speak the heart's words. I cannot find those, so I often give up trying. You speak music's language; I am a musician, but I am still learning. Music speaks to you. Your melody follows it, your rhythms are as basic as our heartbeats and our gait. Your response is a familiar answer to unresolved cadences.

"Eemee!" *I am here, shaking the tambourine, making the cymbals shine, watching the ribbons twirl. I am singing and laughing. I am doing what I love. Here I am, in the music.*

"I hear you, Reva. Eemee."[106]

IDENTIFYING WITH MUSIC

My encounters with Reva have taught me so much about who I am and how much music is a part of who I am. Here are some questions to prompt reflection on your relationship with music:

- What is the music inside you that expresses who you are?
- Is there a piece of music that you relate to emotionally?
- How does it feel when you sing/play/dance to/listen to your favorite music?
- How does music affect your mind/body/spirit?
- When and where does music play a significant role in your day or your life?
- How would you like to introduce more music into your life? Here are some examples:
  - taking lessons
  - attending concerts
  - participating in religious worship and sacred music
  - engaging more actively with music
  - writing and composing
  - improvising
  - playing/singing/dancing
  - sharing music with others
  - being creative
- Are there artists with whom you identify strongly?

IDENTIFYING WITH THE ARTIST

At the time of this writing, Taylor Swift is a phenomenon. Her followers are known as "Swifties," and ticket prices to her Eras Tour concert are rumored to cost as much as $20,000—a bargain, according to *New York Times* reporter Paul Krugman.[107] Suzanne Garfinkle-Crowell is a New York psychiatrist who has found that many of her clients are deeply affected by Swift's authentic voice and not only relate to her stories of heartbreak, bullying, angst, vengeance, pain, and love, but are able to see intense emotions and life experiences dissected before their ears. Swiftmania brings with it a community of listeners who follow these profound musical self-explorations and bond through their love or obsession with real life themes.[108] The fans' appreciation for the beauty of the music and Swift's voice, identification with the artist's stories, and the opportunity to gather together to relive these emotional journeys engender an enormous sense of empathy. They feel seen, heard, embraced, and accompanied.

Australian artist Kylie Minogue created what has become an anthem, a meme, and an overall sensation for the LGBTQ community. Released in advance of Gay Pride Month, June 2023, "Padam Padam" is Minogue's nod to the heartbeat of Paris torch singer Edith Piaf, who recorded her love song by this title in 1951. This recent version has fueled the energy of Pride and forged bonds within and outside of the community.[109] A piece of music like this draws in and welcomes anyone who feels an empathetic bond with its intent or content.

TELLING YOUR STORY

While we can identify with the tales of others, we all have a story (or two) to tell. We don't need to write a complete autobiography or a hit song to capture important life lessons. Our authentic voices convey messages that help us understand ourselves and each other, while we investigate pivotal moments that did or could determine our future.

Think of a time, person, event, encounter, or emotion that had some impact on you or changed your course of action. What did you do? How did it feel? What were you thinking? What would you like others to learn from this? You can create your own anthem or theme song or simply tell your story. You can relive an important moment or envision the future in a vivid dream. You can place yourself at the center of your story or advocate for something you believe in. What would you like to share in your music/story? Here are some tips for composing your way into creating meaningful music:

- Identify an intention, goal, or purpose for your music.
- Expand on this theme in your journal.
- Find a source of inspiration to guide you:
    - a relationship or person
    - nature or a place you love
    - a social issue you feel strongly about
    - self-exploration
    - your spirituality or connection to a life force
    - an activity you enjoy
    - a memory or time in your life
    - an event or milestone
    - a dream or vision of the future
- Focus in on sensations or feelings you want to express by:
    - noticing the tempo of your breath
    - starting to hum
    - moving around or dancing
    - using body percussion or an instrument
- Find your vibe. Give a sound to those feelings by generating a chant or melody.
- Decide upon the instrument(s) that will be your voice (or just use your voice!).
- If you develop the process from narratives or lyrics, you can:
    - use your own words (from journaling or spontaneously produced)
    - substitute your words for existing song lyrics in music you love
    - set a poem, phrase, or story to a melody you create
    - say the words out loud exaggerating the intonation
- If you lead the process from sounds and music, you can:
    - generate them organically from your breath, humming, or singing
    - improvise and play around with musical themes
    - play some chords and develop a harmonic structure
    - start with a rhythm that fits your intention

- Employ a simple song structure, for example:
  - ¤ ABA (first theme, second theme, repetition of first theme)
  - ¤ Verse 1, chorus, verse 2, chorus
  - ¤ Exposition, development, recapitulation (sonata form)
- Take your time with the process and take some breaks to let your ideas simmer.
- Record your experimentation in order to save your ideas.

I hope that you will enjoy experimenting with any of these ideas or create your own way of expressing something important to who you are. There are some great resources for trying your hand at improvisation.[110] Of course, mastering more musical instruments and improving your vocal skills not only provide a broader vocabulary for your story, but also help create that awesome state of being, known as "flow."

LET IT FLOW

Mihayli Csikszentmihalyi wrote a book on flow,[111] which became a bestseller and precursor to new approaches for achieving optimal performance. Flow is that remarkable sweet spot of intense focus, clarity, and confidence that brings a sense of serenity and timelessness that is often expressed as ecstasy. In chapter 3, Bea described the flow of her drumming, and we discussed being "in the groove" with Zen. Now, we focus on the ingredients of this remarkable sensation.

Csikszentmihalyi describes flow as a consequence of demonstrating a high level of skill and mastering a challenging task, where the mind is "stretched to its limits" to achieve something particularly meaningful. For example, playing music that is difficult to learn and performed extremely competently or struggling to find the right sounds for your composition and working hard to make it work can lead to a flow state. But another essential element is the immense pleasure of engaging in this activity, especially after a demanding process.

One outcome of feeling the flow is the sense of wonder that is beyond words. Another is "awe"—that inexplicable something that transcends understanding, even for Dacher Keltner, who wrote a book with that title.[112] Awe can give us a perspective that there is something larger, elusive, and more significant than what we sense in our daily existence. Aesthetic awe has been described as an ultimate humanistic response to something sublime.[113] This expansive state of curiosity is associated with reduced proinflammatory cytokines, affecting the immune system, and linking awe directly to health.[114] Recent research emphasizes how awe engages us in social integration, reduced focus on self, changes in our neurophysiology, and an enhanced sense of meaning.[115] What's more, when we share exceptional musical experiences, we bond together in awe. What better way can there be to improve our overall wellbeing!

CHOOSE AWE

We all have this capability to experience awe, whether it is through art and music, nature, beauty, religion, or whatever else triggers this sensation for you. We can't control it, but we can optimize the presence of awe, when we nurture our natural tendencies to be open and curious about the world around us. I can wait for my local bus with my eye on my watch, while searching around the corner for its arrival. Or I can savor the natural beauty in the trees and houses near the bus stop that I missed in my hundreds of visits to that location. Either alternative results in the arrival of the bus at the same time. But the precise observation of the details surrounding me allows me to attend to some novel and pleasant prerequisites of awe.

We can choose a more awesome path through our lives, but it might be instructive to reflect first on who we are.

WHO ARE YOU?

Like awe, "identity" has multiple meanings. Your name, age, profession, race, gender, political leaning, class, religious belief, and countless other factors may determine your identity. But most of these are characteristics or communities that label you. You too might wish to characterize yourself in these ways, but perhaps the more interesting question is: How do you give expression to these identities?

Bea describes the intersectionality that often makes her feel that she cannot find a place for herself. She speaks about how she is able to integrate her two identities through music:

> My parents are from Sri Lanka, so I grew up surrounded by the sounds of Sri Lankan drumming. I was born and raised on the Upper West Side of Manhattan, so I was also raised in a predominantly Jewish community. Jewish culture and music surrounded me as well. When I grew up, I converted to Judaism, and I'm active in my synagogue community as well as other local and national Jewish organizations. It is interesting to note that there are only 14 million Jews around the world, which is about 0.2 percent of the global population. And there are only about 22 million Sri Lankans in the world, which is about 0.3 percent of the total world population. The intersection of those two populations is minuscule. I am at that intersection....
>
> Being a brown, Jewish woman has its own unique challenges. I recall always being drawn to Judaism, but always being questioned in Jewish spaces. I was not the right color; I did not fit in. Even after my conversion (which, by the way, took years of study), the question of "Are you Jewish?" seemed to follow me everywhere. It was frustrating—and frankly, racist. However, usually once I was in Shabbat services, I was happy to be in synagogue.
>
> The question is "Why?" What was it about Shabbat services that could make me deal with the discomfort of walking through the front door and dealing with people asking me, "Do you belong here?" Well, Shabbat is the Jewish Sabbath—a weekly holiday that offers a break from the hectic pace of the rest of the week. Shabbat begins at sundown on Friday. At my synagogue, the service is full of music and prayer. There is a spirituality that brings me joy.
>
> The prayer that speaks to me the most is the "Sh'ma" prayer.... When I listen to my version of the Sh'ma, I have memories of being with my Sri Lankan family and of being with my Jewish family. The music reminds me that I am both Sri Lankan and Jewish.

Listen to Bea's narrative.

Marjorie is considering a new identity, that of musician:

> I started to teach myself to play the ukulele in April, inspired by a story about an elderly woman who decided to learn to play the keyboard in her nineties. I thought the ukulele seemed like an easy and fun instrument with which to play and sing along. It has been proceeding wonderfully. I took a few lessons on YouTube, and my younger son gave me a few lessons. I am enjoying the ukulele so much, and I'm learning something new almost every day. I like that I am challenging myself, but because the ukulele is not overly difficult, I avoid frustration, and instead I am able to feel a sense of accomplishment and fulfillment. I am also teaching myself not to feel my usual perfectionistic pressure and am instead focusing on the learning experience and the enjoyment. I am finding that playing the ukulele is great stress relief for me. Learning to play an instrument now has been an unbelievably rewarding experience. I may even try the guitar next. I am very excited for these new adventures.

93 Listen to Marjorie's narrative.

Emily is an existential thinker who finds her identity through her violin improvisation.

94 Listen to Emily's improvision.

Here is what she has to say about herself:

> I have been thinking a lot about what it means to be here, be alive. To be a person living amongst others in this world and never have answers as to why we are all here, to begin with. Honestly, it is really painful to be alive, but I continue to realize that the heartaches and the hurt make the joy and love even more beautiful. As a sensitive person, I've spent my life trying to make sense of all the feelings that go through me day to day. I am still trying to figure that out, and I probably never will. I probably will never figure out everything my body feels because there are parts of being alive that the brain can't think its way out of. Sometimes, there is just the art of feeling. Feeling so deeply that nothing makes sense anymore. How could we ever comprehend the true miracle of being human?
>
> I remember a time when I tried so hard to numb out because the feelings were too much. It worked for a little

bit, but it eventually crashed and burned, resulting in more feelings to feel because they never actually went away. So nowadays, I'm feeling feelings in the present but also in the past that I never let out. I am choosing to let my body lead, and it's really scary, but it is what's true. I think living what is true to you is one of the most powerful ways to make meaning.... I let my body lead, and it is a constant practice that isn't always perfect. I will forever be learning how to be at home with myself, and that is where music has played such a significant role in my life. I have been talking a lot about how the brain likes to have answers for everything. It is very similar to my musical journey. The most meaningful music I have made in my life is when I just stop thinking and I start feeling. Music is a channel through which we can express ourselves and our emotions through a universal language that doesn't require an explanation or even words.

The process of writing this instrumental piece started off with simply improvising on my violin. Over a beautiful Lydian chord progression [based on the fourth note of the major scale], I breathed into my instrument and let it sing. The melodies started emerging in my head, and I realized that I had a lot to say. What was meant to be one violin singing over the piano turned into multiple layers of violins that built off of each other. I tend to do this a lot with the music I write, especially when writing string parts. I hear one thing, and it leads me to another voice, and then another. It makes me think about the layers and complexities that life holds. In my experience, being human is never just one thing. Being human holds so many layers, so many emotions, so much depth. And that is where I make meaning.

95 Listen to Emily's full narrative.

Shawn introduces himself through the music that has become the theme song and impetus for his career as an artist.

96 Listen to Shawn's music, "If I Fall."

Here are his lyrics.

"If I Fall" by Shawn

I watched the seasons change and the rain fall down
It was colder then 'cause you were not around
I was just waiting for you to come save me
To pick me up and never blame me

Chorus:

Oh I'm wondering
If I Fall, will you catch me?
Will you lay me down slowly,
To break down the weight of the world on my shoulders?

I watched the seasons change and the snow fall down
It was coldest then 'cause you could not be found
I was still waiting for you to come save me
To pick me up and never blame me

(Chorus)

I'm afraid of it all
I can't escape myself and the storm has come
I watch the waves take control as I wait it out
It's the eye of the storm and the calm to come again

(Chorus)

Shawn talks about the origin of this song.

My name is Shawn Kellner. I am an Army veteran, an artist, and a suicide survivor with a spinal cord injury. I wrote my song "If I Fall" thirteen years ago when I was a young aspiring artist and songwriter traveling the world. The lyrics came out but never meant anything literal to me at the time. I had no idea that years later they would become a note to myself. Following my spinal cord injury, I lost the use of my right arm and I thought I would never play music again. That changed when one day a music therapist at Shirley Ryan AbilityLab in Chicago walked into my recovery room and handed me a small keyboard and a harmonica. He told me that I wasn't done yet. I know now that music has never left me. I am still an artist, and have since become a producer and an engineer. I will be releasing my album *World War Me*, which tells my story, next year. I have realized, as I have recovered mentally and physically, that the best way to share my story is through music. It is my salvation.

Listen to Shawn's story.

97

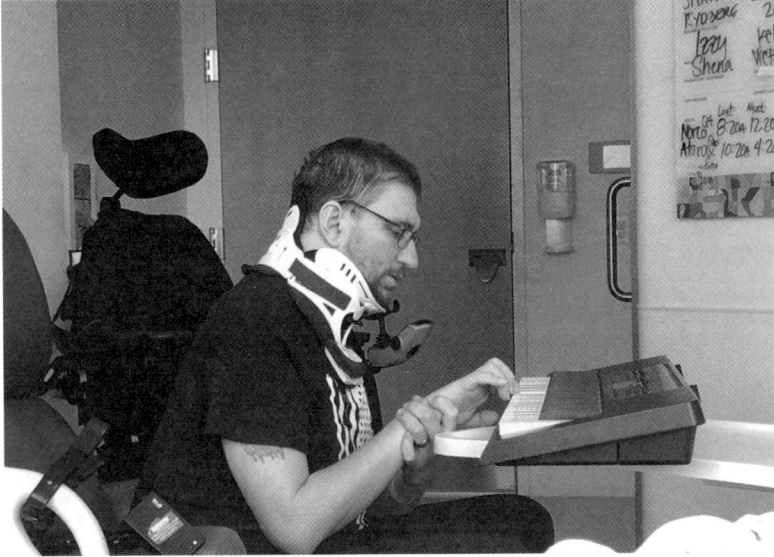

Shawn in Rehabilitation. Photo by Jen Kellner

Hélène identifies strongly with music, and she works with sounds and vibrations to create music that is her essence.

Listen to Hélène's music.

98

Hélène's intention goes far beyond self-understanding. She creates listening circles to enable groups of people to find their music and share their stories.

> The music I create, which directly emanates from a luminous source I have been connected to since I'm a child, is about hope, trust, unconditional love, gratitude. It is one of many testimonies of living on this planet, at this precise moment.
>
> Music, its vibrations and frequencies, is a universal language that goes beyond everything that creates a separation between humans, but also between species and every living being. Its power to connect people, but also to reconnect ourselves to our natural environment, is

immense. It is fundamentally different from other forms of communication....

When I am in a gathering, especially when I feel that people are not very comfortable, I always go for a what I like to call, "listening circle." I propose to each person to choose a song they love, one after another. What happens is magical: people start to open, to talk about the piece they chose, why they love it, when they discovered it—which feelings, emotions, parts of their story it is associated with. And we go on, as a growing spiral. What started as a shy, and even annoying for some, gathering, ends with harmony and union between the participants. We all learn from these types of experiences. Everyone listens to each other without trying to convince; everyone is happy to discover, and know more about each other.

This union through music connects us with something bigger, higher, that goes way beyond the material existence we're experiencing.

99 Listen to Hélène's narrative.

IDENTIFYING WITH NATURE

Gen identifies with nature and the natural world.

100 Listen to Gen's music.

Gen shares the tenets of a profound unity between people and nature, expressed through sound and music:

The connection between humans and the sounds of nature, including the chants of our ancestors, is significant for several reasons. Here are a few key points explaining why this connection is important for human wellbeing:

First, evolutionary bond. Throughout our history as a species, humans have lived in close harmony with nature. Our ancestors relied on the natural environment for sustenance, shelter, and survival. As a result, we have developed an innate bond with the sounds of nature, such as the rustling of leaves, the sound of flowing water, or the melodies of birds. These sounds have become deeply embedded in our collective consciousness and can evoke a sense of calm, connection, and comfort.

Second, stress reduction. Modern life is often filled with stress, noise, and artificial stimuli. The sounds of nature, on the other hand, have been found to have a soothing and calming effect on our minds and bodies. Research has shown that exposure to natural sounds can lower blood pressure, reduce stress hormone levels, and promote relaxation. When we immerse ourselves in the sounds of nature or listen to ancestral chants, we create a therapeutic environment that allows us to unwind, rejuvenate, and heal.

Third, psychological wellbeing. The sounds of nature and ancestral chants can have a profound impact on our mental and emotional wellbeing. They can evoke a sense of connectedness with the world around us, reminding us of our place in the larger web of life. This connection may help alleviate feelings of loneliness, anxiety, and disconnection that are prevalent in modern society. Listening to these sounds can evoke positive emotions, such as awe, wonder, and nostalgia, which contribute to overall psychological wellbeing and can facilitate the healing process.

Fourth, cultural heritage and identity. Ancestral chants carry the essence of our cultural heritage and identity. They are an expression of the wisdom, beliefs, and traditions passed on through generations. By connecting with these chants, we establish a link to our roots and gain a deeper understanding of who we are as individuals and as part of a larger cultural tapestry. This connection to our ancestral sounds can foster a sense of pride, identity, and belonging, which are crucial for personal growth and healing.

Fifth, restoration of balance. In our fast-paced and technology-driven world, we often become disconnected from natural rhythm of life. This disconnection can lead to imbalances in our physical, mental, and spiritual wellbeing. By reconnecting with the sounds of nature and ancestral chants, we can restore that balance and realign ourselves with the natural world. It helps us reconnect with our inner wisdom and intuition, promoting self-awareness and facilitating the healing process.

The connection between humans and the sounds of nature, including ancestral chants, is vital for our wellbeing and healing. It can help reduce stress, promote psychological wellbeing, foster a sense of cultural identity, and restore balance in our lives. By embracing these sounds, we tap into a deep reservoir of wisdom that can guide us on a journey toward healing.

Listen to Gen's narrative and her description of how music can connect us with our ancestors, the earth, and ourselves.

101

David Rothenberg showed us "why birds sing" in his book by that title. In his latest publication, *Nightingales in Berlin: Searching for the Perfect Sound*, he informs us about a contest to find the most beautiful sound in the world.[116] The winner—a soundscape from a Borneo forest with its frog inhabitants, created by Marc Anderson from Sydney, Australia—honors the natural world in his practice of performing music with birds, accompanied by sounds of nature. Bernie Krause developed an entire vocabulary, a "biophony" of environmental sounds, to create *The Great Animal Orchestra*, which I was privileged to experience at the Peabody Essex Museum in Salem, Massachusetts.[117] This installation includes visual spectrograms of animals in seven of the world's habitats, scrolling across the walls of the exhibit, while each animal's vocalizations filter into the room, until the viewer/listener is engulfed in this natural harmony. Krause reminds us of the origins of music within the immense soundscape of nature. He records the consonant sounds of healthy ecosystems and the chaos of environments under stress, and produces a symphony of the world.

Nature lets us know that the music we create is based on natural sounds that we may hear, but not necessarily heed or honor. Whether you live in a bustling city or in a remote area off the map, there are sounds everywhere. Have you listened to the wind lately? Have you heard what your environment is telling you?

CODA

As I reflect on these stories, I glean the uniqueness of each artist and storyteller. I see their self-reflections in the music, and I recognize their best selves in the flow of narrative and musical phrases. The music is honest; the expressions are authentic.

It does not matter if we find ourselves in the music or through the music. What is important is that we are true to ourselves in the process and seek to express a part of our highest selves. When you tell

CHAPTER 10

See the World

your story through sound and song, you find yourself inside a theme song all your own. Who are you?

It's your turn to create the intention for this chapter in your life. You have listened, learned, and read how music can contribute to wellness, resilience, and happiness. You have seen how music has served others in daily life and in dire circumstances. Yet there is something about music that goes beyond these personal applications. While the stories of this book's contributors demonstrate ways to make life more meaningful, there is even more to music. Flow, awe, wonder, transformation, and transcendence are possible.

- How will music enhance your comfort, motivation, energy, creativity, and spirit?

- Will you be able to see the reflection, images and memories, the other, and the self through engaging with music?

- Will you create a soundtrack for your life and make music more a part of your future?

- How will you craft opportunities for these larger than life experiences amidst your quotidian routine or when you are casting doubt on your abilities or your potential?

PLAY FOR PEACE

In September, 2004, the Steinway Peace Piano arrived in Boston, after its inaugural performance by UNICEF Goodwill Ambassador Lang Lang and other notable pianists in New York City. This gorgeous concert grand was a replica of the piano featured at the 1939 World's Fair, which is currently on exhibit at the Smithsonian Institution.

Built from blond wood, it is decorated with a band of flags of 195 nations, and two doves perched on a laurel branch, replacing gold eagles on the original piano.

On this first stop of its world tour to benefit UNICEF, Steinway representative Vivian Handis decided that it would be fitting to host a special physicians' benefit concert to feature this remarkable new instrument. I was honored to be invited to perform amongst a group of eminent doctors who are also pianists. I decided to play the *Fantasy in D Minor* by Mozart.

I learned this showpiece when I was about eleven years old. At that age, I had an inkling of the magic of Mozart, but I had no idea that I would feel his presence so viscerally that night. At that concert, Mozart helped clothe, feed, and shelter children around the world as the Peace Piano Concert benefited the cause of UNICEF.

I looked at the keyboard and reached out, laying my hands on the gleaming surface. The first note buzzed, and I was carried into it. We resonated amongst the taller-than-human-size strings that lay at the piano's heart. We bubbled up in waves of sound and burst into the sounding board. We careened into the room at diverse angles, pulsing each listener in a different tempo. When we reached the walls in a split-second eternity, we bounced back, like a child's ball. I toyed with some eighth notes, squeezing the sixty-fourth note run into a hundred-note crash. All the while in a dream state, this performer was letting the composer do the work. This performer was only the medium. Three hundred years of vibrations from Mozart's fantasy led the way and played the piece. I needed only to stay inside it.

A frenzied cadenza fizzled into a melody fit for a baby doll. The keys crystalized, and I heard sparkles. While the piece seemed to play itself, I was back in a time when I first learned to play Mozart, when scales and arpeggios were my daily bread, and Mozart was an oddly spelled name. My full attention was on my fingers then—their shape and pressure, their stepping motion from one to another, their direction and line of flow, their balance and kinesthetics to make this all possible. My full attention was on too many variables to count, too complex a process to describe, too much for a young child to consciously coordinate. Then, hours of practice, years of study, multiple coaches, more rehearsals, repeated thousands of times prepared me to play the *Fantasy in D Minor* at this remarkable event.

All this and decades of experience interacting with the world—listening, watching, feeling, smelling, touching, tasting, moving through it—helped me perform this feat. My physical body sat back to maintain balance and control. The rest of me was somewhere between the past and future. Finally, the last note intoned complete resolution. I rose and bent to acknowledge the applause. But it was not for me. It was for Mozart and the millions of interpreters of this famous fantasy, teachers and tutors and mentors and masters and

M. Steinert & Sons
STEINWAY & OTHER PIANOS OF DISTINCTION

unicef

STEINWAY & SONS

A Physician's Benefit Concert for UNICEF
featuring
The Steinway and Sons Peace Piano

September 21, 2004 at 7 pm   Steinert Hall, Boston, MA

Fantasy in D minor, K. 397	Dr. Suzanne Hanser, piano	Mozart
Suite in D minor, G. 108 *Allemande* *Courante* *Sarabande* *Gigue*	Dr. William Coukos, piano	Handel
Impromptus, Op. 90, Numbers 1 and 2 La Cathedral Engloutie from Preludes Bk. 1	Dr. Ernest War, piano	Schubert Debussy
Prelude and Fugue in C-sharp Major from WTC, Bk. II, No. 3 Sonata in F. Major, K.531 Intermezzo in B-flat minor, Op. 117, No.2	Dr. Frank Bunn, piano	Bach Scarlatti Brahms
Serenity	Dr. Maria Hernandez, piano	Maria Hernandez
Blues For The Children of the World Somewhere Over The Rainbow Prelude No. 2 in C-sharp minor	Dr. Eli Newberger, piano and tuba	Eli Newberger Arlen Gershwin

Steinway Peace Piano Concert Program. Photo by Vivian Handis loved ones, and for the past and the future of children everywhere, and for Peace.

Several years ago, Joshua Bell played the Franck violin sonata in my friend's living room. My friend had won a silent auction bid to have a recital for a dozen of her closest friends, and I was glad to have been included as a guest. So, Joshua Bell and his pianist played just for us. As far as I was concerned, they were playing just for me. Joshua Bell was a budding virtuoso, and I was a starstruck fan. The pianist was demure, but stunning, ready for his cue, his breath held in anticipation. I waited with him, wondering how long I could hold my breath.

The sonata began, and I breathed along, while my heart beat in intimate rapidity. Soon, I felt my blood pressure deflating. As I was swinging between the melodic shifts of excitement and comfort, I recognized my favorite theme. There, I found the notes reaching, descending, reaching, descending, reaching again, defining yearning. As the pitches stretched upward, I was seeking, looking heavenward, only to plummet and reach again with the music, continuing the cycle, the cycle of life, my most private struggle, my most desperate inner momentum. I was moving toward the future, to a place I could not know. The music and my desire to understand where I was going propelled me ahead, but I tarried, forward and back, with the music, always with the music, in hope and fear, in desire and dread.

It was exhausting and exhilarating. I was sweating from the tension, or was it the harmony? And then, before I was ready, it resolved. I heard the audience exhale together with contagious optimism. Our pilgrimage ended on the tonic, the tonal center of its scale. We were in a familiar place, home at last. Everyone applauded and cried.

"Magnificent," one cheered.

"Such beauty," said another.

"A God-like feat" from someone else.

But these words were insufficient to explain the depth of our experience. Something happened to us, something important, something beyond the capabilities of mere mortals. What we heard, what we experienced, was more than the up-and-down movement of musical notation from two practiced musicians. It happened inside the interplay of wavering vibrato and thick chords, the competition of form and freedom embodied in two robust bodies, the combination of two timbres intertwining as though they were embracing lovers. Our sensations lacked vocabulary. But all of the eyes in my friend's living room spoke one thing for sure: we glimpsed our future, and it was good.

MUSIC FOR MORE THAN WELLNESS

While writing this book, I was privileged to hear the world première of *Zhiân* for orchestra, by Iman Habibi, at Tanglewood, the summer home of the Boston Symphony Orchestra. Habibi was born in Tehran, Iran, during the Iran-Iraq war, and experienced the oppression of basic freedoms and injustices, while being surrounded by the imprisonment and death of many of his fellow Iranians. "Zhiân" is the Kurdish given name of Mahsa Amini, whose death along with other young women sparked massive protests. The word Zhiân, meaning "life" in Kurdish and "indignant" or "formidable" in Persian, became a revolutionary chant and the theme for this very moving music. Habibi wrote the piece in solidarity and dedication to the people of Iran, educating us listeners about their tragic fate, and moving us into the chaos of life of Iran.

On the same program was Jessie Montgomery's *Five Freedom Songs*, traditional Black spirituals for voice, percussion, and string orchestra. Based on *Slave Songs of the United States*,[118] this music struck the audience with its merciless accounts of oppression juxtaposed with spiritual salvation. I could hear the clanging of chains amongst the African drums in the musical score.

These gripping examples affected us listeners in ways that words could never communicate. Our bodies vibrated with the music, as we were taken far away from our comfortable seats in the concert hall.

THIS TIME IN HISTORY

As the world begins to reawaken from the sleep induced by COVID-19, awareness of injustice and inhumanity, discrimination, political unrest and war, health disparities and inequality, and threats to climate, resulting in record-breaking heat waves and wildfires, are keen and palpable. Throughout history, music has brought us together. Now, perhaps, it is time to sing the songs that can move us forward, to play our instruments to express both outrage and hope, and to compose music that communicates the important messages for our time and for our future. Wherever we are in the world, whatever language we speak, whenever we have something to say, music can be a courier of unity and peace. Let each of us play and sing our part.

We are at a pivotal time in our history. In *The Structure of Scientific Revolutions*, Thomas Kuhn writes about how real change comes about in science.[119] He says that the greatest paradigm shifts— changes in the way we think about and approach things—do not occur with discovery building on discovery, in a systematic way. Rather, significant changes happen when our theories fall apart or when we witness something totally unexpected. I like to think that when I feel that the world I know is crashing down, I can build a future that is new and better than anything it could have been before.

Dean Keith Simonton examined creativity from a historical perspective, investigating 127 twenty-year periods in Europe, India, China, and the Islamic world, from 700 BCE to 1839 CE.[120] He found that political fragmentation was a strong predictor of periods of societal creativity. Cultural diversification also helped lead change from disequilibrium to synthesis of ideas. So there is a chance that a unified force can activate our creativity to forge a better world.

It was after the murder of President John F. Kennedy that Leonard Bernstein told us to make music in response to violence.[121]

This is my hope for you and for us.

NOTES

INTRODUCTION

1. Hanser, S. B. (2010). *Integrative health through music therapy: Accompanying the journey from illness to wellness.* London: Palgrave Macmillan.

2. Thaut, M. H. (2008). *Rhythm, music and the brain: Scientific foundations and clinical applications.* New York: Routledge.

3. Thaut, M. H., & Abiru, M. (2010). Rhythmic auditory stimulation in rehabilitation of movement disorders: A review of current research. *Music Perception*, 27(4), 263–269.

4. National Wellness Institute. (n.d.). *Six dimensions of wellness.* Retrieved June 18, 2023, from **https://nationalwellness.org/ resources/six-dimensions-of-wellness/**

5. National Institute of Mental Health. (n.d.). *I am so stressed out!* [Fact Sheet]. Retrieved June 18, 2023 from **https://www.nimh.nih.gov/ health/publications/so-stressed-out-fact-sheet**

6. McGonigal, K. (2015). *The upside of stress.* New York: Avery Press, p. xxi.

7. For more information about the autonomic nervous system, see:

    Cleveland Clinic. (n.d.). *Autonomic nervous system.* Retrieved June 18, 2023, from **https://my.clevelandclinic.org/health/ body/23273-autonomic-nervous-system**

8. Karatsoreos, I. N., & McEwen, B. S. (2011). Psychobiological allostasis: resistance, resilience and vulnerability. *Trends in Cognitive Sciences, 15*(12), P576–584. **https://doi.org/10.1016/j.tics.2011.10.005**

9. Gilbert, E. (2015). *Big magic: Creative living beyond fear.* New York: Riverhead Books.

10. United Nations Sustainable Development Solutions Network. (n.d.). *World Happiness Report.* Retrieved June 18, 2023, from **https://worldhappiness.report/**

11. Colston, P. (2023, April 1). The Finnish secret to happiness? Knowing when you have enough. *The New York Times.*

12. Gee, D. (2022). Five essentials of music career success. **https://www.berklee.edu/careers/essentialsofsuccess.html**

13. Silva, C. (2017, June 4). The millennial obsession with self-care. *NPR Health.* **https://www.npr.org/2017/06/04/531051473/ the-millennial-obsession-with-self-care**

14. Rennis, L., McNamara, G., Seidel, E., & Shneyderman, Y. (2015). Google It! Urban community college students' use of the internet to obtain self-care and personal health information. *College Student Journal, 49*(3), 414–426.

15. Neff, K., & Germer, C. (2018). *The mindful self-compassion workbook: A proven way to accept yourself, build inner strength, and thrive.* New York: Guilford Press.

16. Ogden, J. (2013). Creative writing and your brain. *Psychology Today.* **https://www.psychologytoday.com/us/blog/ trouble-in-mind/201304/creative-writing-and-your-brain**

CHAPTER 1

17. See these references on music interventions:

  Bernatzky, G., Presch, M., Anderson, M., & Panksepp, J. (2011). Emotional foundations of music as a non-pharmacological pain management tool in modern medicine. *Neuroscience & Biobehavioral Reviews, 35*(9), 1989–1999.

  Bradt, J., Dileo, C., & Shim, M. (2013). Music interventions for preoperative anxiety. *Cochrane Database of Systematic Reviews,* (6). **https://doi.org/10.1002/14651858.CD006908.pub2**

  Daniel, E. (2016). Music used as anti-anxiety intervention for patients during outpatient procedures: A review of the literature. *Complementary Therapies in Clinical Practice, 22,* 21–23.

  Yinger, O. S., & Gooding, L. F. (2015). A systematic review of music-based interventions for procedural support. *Journal of Music Therapy, 52*(1), 1–77.

18. Loewy, J. (2015). NICU music therapy: Song of kin as critical lullaby in research and practice. *Annals of the New York Academy of Sciences, 1337*(1), 178–185.

19. Loewy, J., Stewart, K., Dassler, A. M., Telsey, A., & Homel, P. (2013). The effects of music therapy on vital signs, feeding, and sleep in premature infants. *Pediatrics, 131*(5), 902–918.

20. Hanser, S. B., & Mandel, S. E. (2010). *Manage your stress and pain through music.* Boston: Berklee Press.

21. Schullian, D. M., & Schoen, M. (Eds.) (1948). *Music and Medicine,* Subseries 1.8, Box: 101, Folder: 20. Records of the American Music Therapy Association, MMTA. CSU Libraries Archives & Special Collections. **https://archives.colostate.edu/repositories/2/archival_objects/19162**

22. Vuilleumier, P., & Trost, W. (2015). Music and emotions: From enchantment to entrainment. *Annals of the New York Academy of Sciences, 1337*(1), 212–222.

23. Mezuk, B., Maust, D., & Zivin, K. (2022). A response to the President's call to support public mental health. *American Journal of Preventive Medicine, 63*(4), 660–663.

24. See these studies on sleep:

    Clement-Carbonell, V., Portilla-Tamarit, I., Rubio-Aparicio, M., & Madrid-Valero, J. J. (2021). Sleep quality, mental and physical health: A differential relationship. *International Journal of Environmental Research and Public Health, 18*(2), 460.

    Cordi, M. J., Ackermann, S., & Rasch, B. (2019). Effects of relaxing music on healthy sleep. *Scientific Reports, 9,* 1–9.

    Fondell, E., Axelsson, J., Franck, K., Ploner, A., Lekander, M., & Gaines, H. (2011). Short natural sleep is associated with higher T cell and lower NK cell activities. *Brain, Behavior, and Immunity, 25*(7), 1367–1375.

    Huang, B-H., del Pozo Cruz, B., Teixeira-Pinto, A., Cistulli, P. A., & Stamatakis, E. (2023). Influence of poor sleep on cardiovascular disease-free life expectancy: A multi-resource-based population cohort study. *BMC Medicine, 21*(75). **https://doi.org/10.1186/s12916-023-02732-x**

    Suzuki, H., Savitz, J., Teague, T. K., Gandhapudi, S. K., Tan, C., ... & Bodurka, J. (2017). Altered populations of natural killer cells, cytotoxic T lymphocytes, and regulatory T cells in major depressive disorder: Association with sleep disturbance. *Brain, Behavior, and Immunity, 66,* 193–200.

25. Scott, A. J., Webb, T. L., Martyn-St. James, M., Rowse, G., & Weich, S. (2021). Improving sleep quality leads to better mental health: A meta-analysis of randomised controlled trials. *Sleep Medicine Reviews, 60*, 101556.

26. For more on sleep in general, see:

    Walker, M. (2017). *Why we sleep.* New York: Scribner.

27. See these references on music's effects on sleep:

    DeNiet, G., Tiemens, B., Lendejeijer, B., & Hutschemaekers, G. (2009). Music-assisted relaxation to improve sleep quality: Meta-analysis. *Journal of Advanced Nursing, 65*(7), 1356–1364.

    Jespersen, K. V., Koenig, J., Jennum, P., & Vuust, P. (2015). Music for insomnia in adults. *Cochrane Database of Systematic Reviews*, (8). **https://doi.org/10.1002/14651858.CD010459.pub2**

    Scarratt, R. J., Heggli, O. A., Vuust, P., & Jespersen, K. V. (2023). The audio features of sleep music: Universal and subgroup characteristics. *PloS one, 18*(1), e0278813. **https://doi.org/10.1371/journal.pone.0278813**

    Dickson, G. T., & Schubert, E. (2020). Music on prescription to aid sleep quality: A literature review. *Frontiers in Psychology, 11*, 1695. **https://doi.org/10.3389/fpsyg.2020.01695**

28. See these references on silence:

    Wasserstein, D. J. (1999). *A west-east puzzle: On the history of the proverb "Speech is silver, silence is golden."* University Park, PA: Eisenbrauns.

    Arazi, A., Sadan, J., & Wasserstein, D. J. (Eds.). (1999). *Compilation and creation in Adab and Luġa: Studies in memory of Naphtali Kinberg (1948–1997).* University Park, PA: Eisenbrauns.

CHAPTER 2

29. Ellis, H. (1898). *Affirmations* (1st ed.). London: Constable & Company, p. vii.

30. Brach, T. (2004). *Radical acceptance: Embracing your life with the heart of a Buddha.* New York: Bantam Books.

31. Sherman, D. K. (2013). Self-affirmation: Understanding the effects. *Social and Personality Psychology Compass, 7*(11), 834–845.

32. See these references on self-affirmation:

> McQueen, A., & Klein, W. M. (2006). Experimental manipulations of self-affirmation: A systematic review. *Self and Identity, 5*(4), 289–354.

> Critcher, C. R., Dunning, D., & Armor, D. A. (2010). When self-affirmations reduce defensiveness: Timing is key. *Personality and Social Psychology Bulletin, 36*(7), 947–959.

33. Alexander, L. (2021). Do positive affirmations work? Here's what experts say. *Cleveland Clinic HealthEssentials.* **https://health.clevelandclinic.org/do-positive-affirmations-work/**

34. See these references on yoga:

> Cope, S. (2006). *The wisdom of yoga: A seeker's guide to extraordinary living.* New York: Bantam Books.

> Simpson, D. (2021). *The truth of yoga: A comprehensive guide to yoga's history, texts, philosophy, and practices.* New York: Northpoint Press.

> Michalopoulus, D. (n.d.). The future of Yoga. *Yoga Journal.* **https://www.yogajournal.com/lifestyle/yoga-trends/**

35. Paul, R. (2006). *The yoga of sound: Tapping the hidden power of music and chant.* Novato, CA: New World Library.

36. Gannon, S., & Life, D. (2002). *Jivamukti yoga: Practices for liberating body and soul.* New York: Ballantine Books.

37. See these references on chant:

> Amin, A., Kumar, S. S., Rajagopalan, A., Rajan, S., Mishra, F., ..., & Amin, A. (2016). Beneficial effects of OM chanting on depression, anxiety, stress and cognition in elderly women with hypertension. *Indian Journal of Clinical Anatomy and Physiology, 3*(3), 253–255.

> Gao, J., Leung, H. K., Wu, B. W. Y., Skouras, S., & Sik, H. H. (2019). The neurophysiological correlates of religious chanting. *Scientific Reports, 9*(1), 4262. **https://doi.org/10.1038/s41598-019-40200-w**

> Kenny, M., Bernier, R., & DeMartini, C. (2005). Chant and be happy: The effects of chanting on respiratory function and

general well-being in individuals diagnosed with depression. *International Journal of Yoga Therapy, 15*(1), 61–64. **https://doi.org/10.17761/ijyt.15.1.878t7l2441p80h17**

38. Premal, D. (2016). *Gayatri Mantra.* [recorded by D. Premal.] **https://www.youtube.com/watch?v=yQjHSIHPJfw**

39. Arien, A. (2010). *The four-fold way: Walking the paths of the warrior, teacher, healer, and visionary.* San Francisco: Harper One.

40. Playing for Change. (n.d.). *We inspire the world.* Retrieved June 18, 2023, from **https://www.playingforchange.com**

41. Stevens, C. (2012). *Music medicine: The science of healing yourself with sound.* Boulder, CO: Sounds True.

42. Morinville, A., Miranda, D., & Gaudreau, P. (2013). Music listening motivation is associated with global happiness in Canadian late adolescents. *Psychology of Aesthetics, Creativity, and the Arts, 7*(4), 384–390. **https://doi.org/10.1037/a0034495**

CHAPTER 3

43. TooFab. (2020, August 14). *Relatable songs written about the pandemic that will cover all your quarantine emotions.* Retrieved June 18, 2023, from **https://toofab.com/2020/08/14/26-relatable-songs-written-about-the-pandemic-that-will-cover-all-your-quarantine-emotions/**

44. See these references on catharsis:

    Sandhu P. (2015). Step aside, Freud: Josef Breuer is the true father of modern psychotherapy. *Scientific American 2015.*

    Nichols, M. P., & Efran, J. S. (1985). Catharsis in psychotherapy: A new perspective. *Psychotherapy: Theory, Research, Practice, Training, 22*(1), 46–58. **https://doi.org/10.1037/h0088525**

45. Bylsma, L. M., Croon, M. A., Vingerhoets, A. J. J. M., & Rattenberg, J. (2011). When and for whom does crying improve mood? A daily diary study of 1004 crying episodes. *Journal of Research in Personality, 45*(4), 385–392. **https://doi.org/10.1016/j.jrp.2011.04.007**

46. Buckingham, V. (2002, September 8). My side of the story: Terrorism and security were not the only concerns at Logan Airport during the September 11 crisis. Political opportunism and finger-pointing also had their day. *Boston Globe Magazine.*

47. Adibah, S. M., & Zakaria, M. (2015). The efficacy of expressive arts therapy in the creation of catharsis in counselling. *Mediterranean Journal of Social Sciences, 6*(6 S1), 298.

48. Diallo, Y., & Hall, M. (1989). *The healing drum: African wisdom teachings.* Rochester, VT: Destiny Books.

49. Fancourt, D., Perkins, R., Ascenso, S., Carvalho, L. A., Steptoe, A., & Williamon, A. (2016). Effects of group drumming interventions on anxiety, depression, social resilience and inflammatory immune response among mental health service users. *PloS one, 11*(3), e0151136.

50. See these references on drumming:

Smith, C., Viljoen, J. T., & McGeachie, L. (2014). African drumming: A holistic approach to reducing stress and improving health? *Journal of Cardiovascular Medicine, 15*(6), 441–446.

Wood, L., Ivery, P., Donovan, R., & Lambin, E. (2013). "To the beat of a different drum": Improving the social and mental wellbeing of at-risk young people through drumming. *Journal of Public Mental Health, 12*(2), 70–79.

51. Schrock, K. (2009). Why music moves us. *Scientific American Mind, 20*(4), 32–37.

52. Pashman, S. E. (2014). When the music moves you: Revisiting the classics in the company of neuroscience. *Journal of Music and Dance, 4*(2), 10–24.

53. Hodges, D. A., & Wilkins, R. W. (2015). How and why does music move us? Answers from psychology and neuroscience. *Music Educators Journal, 101*(4), 41–47.

54. See these references on music and emotion:

Juslin, P. (2019). *Musical emotions explained: Unlocking the secrets of musical affect.* Oxford, UK: Oxford University Press.

Korsavoa-Kreyn, M. (2022). *Music and emotion: Embodied cognition and images of time.* Independently published.

Levitin, D. J. (2016). *This is your brain on music: The science of a human obsession.* New York: Dutton.

Sacks, O. (2007). *Musicophilia: Tales of music and the brain.* New York: Vintage Books.

55. Terry, P. C., Karageorghis, C. I., Curran, M. L., Martin, O. V., & Parsons-Smith, R. L. (2020). Effects of music in exercise and sport: A meta-analytic review. *Psychological Bulletin, 146*(2), 91–117. **https://doi.org/10.1037/bul0000216**

56. Nakamura, P. M., Pereira, G., Papini, C. B., Nakamura, F. Y., & Kokubun, E. (2010). Effects of preferred and nonpreferred music on continuous cycling exercise performance. *Perceptual and Motor Skills, 110*(1), 257–264.

57. Murrock, C. J., & Higgins, P. A. (2009). The theory of music, mood and movement to improve health outcomes. *Journal of Advanced Nursing, 65*(10), 2249–2257.

58. Clark, I. N., Baker, F. A., & Taylor, N. F. (2016). The modulating effects of music listening on health-related exercise and physical activity in adults: A systematic review and narrative synthesis. *Nordic Journal of Music Therapy, 25*(1), 76–104.

59. Chappell, K., Redding, E., Crickmay, U., Stancliffe, R., Jobbins, V., & Smith, S. (2021). The aesthetic, artistic and creative contributions of dance for health and wellbeing across the lifecourse: A systematic review. *International Journal of Qualitative Studies on Health and Well-Being, 16*(1), 1950891.

60. For more on dance and health, see these references:

    Pickard, A., & Risner, D. (2020). Dance, health and wellbeing special issue. *Research in Dance Education, 21*(2), 225–227.

    American Dance Therapy Association. (n.d.). *What is dance/ movement therapy?* Retrieved June 18, 2023, from: **https://www.adta.org/**

61. Koch, S. C., Riege, R. F., Tisborn, K., Biondo, J., Martin, L., & Beelmann, A. (2019). Effects of dance movement therapy and dance on health-related psychological outcomes. A meta-analysis update. *Frontiers in Psychology, 10,* 1806.

62. See these references on dance and health:

    Goldsmith, S., & Kokolakakis, T. (2021). A cost-effectiveness evaluation of "Dance to Health": A dance-based falls prevention exercise programme in England. *Public Health, 198,* 17–21.

    Mattle, M., Chocano-Bedoya, P. O., Fischbacher, M., Meyer, U., Abderhalden, L. A., ... & Bischoff-Ferrari, H. A. (2020).

Association of dance-based mind-motor activities with falls and physical function among healthy older adults: A systematic review and meta-analysis. *JAMA Network Open, 3*(9), e2017688–e2017688.

63. Niranjan, V., Tarantino, G., Kumar, J., Cassidy, N., Galvin, L., ... & O'Regan, A. (2022). Dancing for health and wellbeing: A feasibility study of examining health impacts of online dancing among pulmonary fibrosis patients. *International Journal of Environmental Research and Public Health, 19*(20), 13510.

64. Madison, G., Gouyon, F., Ullén, F., & Hörnström, K. (2011). Modeling the tendency for music to induce movement in humans: First correlations with low-level audio descriptors across music genres. *Journal of Experimental Psychology: Human Perception and Performance, 37*(5), 1578–1594. **https://doi.org/10.1037/a0024323**

65. See these references on neurologic music therapy:

    Thaut, M. H., & Abiru, M. (2010). Rhythmic auditory stimulation in rehabilitation of movement disorders: A review of current research. *Music Perception, 27*(4), 263–269.

    Thaut, M., & Hoemberg, V. (Eds.). (2014). *Handbook of neurologic music therapy.* Oxford, UK: Oxford University Press.

66. Stiles, M. (interpreter) (2021). *The Yoga Sutras of Patanjali.* Newburyport, MA: Weiser Books.

67. Hanser, S. B., Larson, S. C., & O'Connell, A. S. (1983). The effect of music on relaxation of expectant mothers during labor. *Journal of Music Therapy, 20*(2), 50–58.

68. Balban, M. Y., Neri, E., Kogon, M. M., Weed, L., Nouriani, B., ... & Huberman, A. D. (2023). Brief structured respiration practices enhance mood and reduce physiological arousal. *Cell Reports Medicine*, 100895.

CHAPTER 4

69. For more on the philosophy of science, see:

    Fuller, S. (2004). *Kuhn vs. Popper: The struggle for the soul of science.* New York: Columbia University Press.

70. For more on everyday creativity, see:

    Richards, R. (2007). Everyday creativity: Our hidden potential. In R. Richards & M. Csikszentmihalyi (Eds.). *Everyday creativity and new views of human nature: Psychological, social, and spiritual perspectives*, (pp. 25–53). Washington, D.C.: American Psychological Association.

Richards, R. (2010). Everyday creativity: Process and way of life—Four key issues. In J. C. Kaufman & R. J. Sternberg (Eds.), *The Cambridge handbook of creativity* (pp. 189–215). Cambridge, UK: Cambridge University Press. **https://doi.org/10.1017/CBO9780511763205.013**

Rubin, R. (2023). *The creative act: A way of being.* New York: Penguin Press.

71. May, R. (1975). *The courage to create.* New York: Norton & Co.

72. Silvia, P. J., Beaty, R. E., Nusbaum, E. C., Eddington, K. M., Levin-Aspenson, H., & Kwapil, T. R. (2014). Everyday creativity in daily life: An experience-sampling study of "little c" creativity. *Psychology of Aesthetics, Creativity, and the Arts, 8*(2), 183–188. **https://doi.org/10.1037/a0035722**

73. Baas, M., De Dreu, C. K., Nijstad, B. A.(2008). A meta-analysis of 25 years of mood-creativity research: hedonic tone, activation, or regulatory focus? *Psychological Bulletin. 134*(6), 779–806. **doi: 10.1037/a0012815. PMID: 18954157**

74. Csikszentmihalyi, M. (1996). *Creativity: The psychology of discovery and invention.* New York: HarperCollins.

75. Goldberg, E. (2018). *Creativity: The human brain in the age of innovation.* Oxford, UK: Oxford University Press.

76. Walker, R. (2019). *The art of noticing: 131 ways to spark creativity, find inspiration, and discover joy in the everyday.* New York: Alfred A. Knopf.

CHAPTER 5

77. Gilman, D. C., Peck, H. T., & Colby, F. M., (Eds.). (1905). Harmonium. *New International Encyclopedia* (1st ed.). New York: Dodd, Mead.

78. Harel, K., Czamanski-Cohen, J., & Turjeman, N. (2021). The spiritual experience of Sufi whirling Dervishes: Rising above the separation and duality of this world. *The Arts in Psychotherapy, 75*, 101831.

79. Kaivalya, A. (2014). *Sacred sound: Discovering the myth and meaning of mantra and kirtan.* Novato, CA: New World Library.

80. Cameron, J. (1992, 2002, 2016). *The artist's way: A spiritual path to higher creativity.* New York: Penguin Random House.

81. Wooten, V. L. (2021). *The spirit of music.* New York: Vintage Books.

82. Lauzon, P. L. (2020). Music and spirituality: Explanations and implications for music therapy. *British Journal of Music Therapy, 34*(1), 30–38. **https://doi.org/10.1177/1359457520908263**

83. See these references on liminality:

> Brown, K. B. (2007). Introduction: Liminality and the social location of musicians. *Twentieth–Century Music, 3*(1), 5–12.

> Turner, V. (1979). Frame, flow and reflection: Ritual and drama as public liminality. *Japanese Journal of Religious Studies, 6*(4), 465–499.

CHAPTER 6

84. DeNora, T. (2016). *Music asylums: Wellbeing through music in everyday life.* Abingdon, Oxon, UK: Routledge.

85. Neff, K., & Germer, C. (2018). *The mindful self-compassion workbook: A proven way to accept yourself, build inner strength, and thrive.* New York: Guilford Press.

86. Emmons, R. A., & McCullough, M. E. (2003). Counting blessings versus burdens: An experimental investigation of gratitude and subjective well-being in daily life. *Journal of Personality and Social Psychology, 84*(2), 377–389. **https://doi.org/10.1037/0022-3514.84.2.377**

87. Dickens, L. R. (2017). Using gratitude to promote positive change: A series of meta-analyses investigating the effectiveness of gratitude interventions. *Basic and Applied Social Psychology, 39*(4), 193–208. **doi: 10.1080/01973533.2017.1323638**

For more on gratitude, see these references:

> Emmons, R. A., & Mishra, A. (2011). Why gratitude enhances well-being: What we know, what we need to know. In K. M. Sheldon, T. B. Kashdan, & M. F. Steger (Eds.), *Designing positive psychology: Taking stock and moving forward* (pp. 248–262). Oxford, UK: Oxford University Press. **https://doi.org/10.1093/acprof:oso/9780195373585.003.0016**

> Guengerich, G. (2020). *The way of gratitude.* New York: Random House.

Jacobs, A. J. (2019). *Thanks a thousand: A gratitude journey.* New York: TED Books, Simon & Shuster.

88. Brach, T. (2019). *Radical compassion.* New York: Viking.

CHAPTER 7

89. Graff-Radford, J., & Lunde, A. M. (Eds.). *Mayo Clinic on Alzheimer's disease and other dementias.* New York: Mayo Clinic Press.

90. Jacobsen, J. H., Stelzer, J., Fritz, T. H., Chételat, G., La Joie, R., & Turner, R. (2015). Why musical memory can be preserved in advanced Alzheimer's disease. *Brain, 138*(8), 2438–2450.

91. Bonny, H. L. (1989). Sound as symbol: Guided imagery and music in clinical practice. *Music Therapy Perspectives, 6(1),* 7–10. **https://doi.org/10.1093/mtp/6.1.7**

    For more on contemporary uses of Guided Imagery and Music and research, see:

    Grocke, D. E., & Moe, T. (Eds.). (2015). *Guided imagery and music (GIM) and music imagery methods for individual and group therapy.* London: Jessica Kingsley.

    Grocke, D. E. (2010). An overview of research in the Bonny Method of Guided Imagery and Music. *Voices: A World Forum for Music Therapy 10*(3). **https://doi.org/10.15845/voices.v10i3.340**

92. Nilson, J. (2010). Albert Einstein: Imagination is more important than knowledge. *The Saturday Evening Post.* **https://www.saturdayeveningpost.com/2010/03/ imagination-important-knowledge/**

CHAPTER 8

93. Kazdin, A. E., & Wilcoxon, L. A. (1976). Systematic desensitization and nonspecific treatment effects: A methodological evaluation. *Psychological Bulletin, 83,* 729–758.

94. Moss, H., Lynch, J., & O'Donoghue, J. (2018). Exploring the perceived health benefits of singing in a choir: An international cross-sectional mixed-methods study. *Perspectives in Public Health, 138*(3), 160–168.

95. Keeler, J. R., Roth, E. A., Neuser, B. L., Spitsbergen, J. M., Waters, D. J. M., & Vianney, J. M. (2015). The neurochemistry and social flow of singing: bonding and oxytocin. *Frontiers in human neuroscience, 9.* **https://doi.org/10.3389/fnhum.2015.00518**

96. Kreutz, G., Bongard, S., Rohrmann, S., Hodapp, V., & Grebe, D. (2004). Effects of choir singing or listening on secretory immunoglobulin A, cortisol, and emotional state. *Journal of Behavioral Medicine, 27,* 623–635.

97. Fancourt, D., Williamon, A., Carvalho, L. A., Steptoe, A., Dow, R., & Lewis, I. (2016). Singing modulates mood, stress, cortisol, cytokine and neuropeptide activity in cancer patients and carers. *ecancer, 10.* **doi: 10.3332/ecancer.2016.631**

98. Gereben, J. (2011). *Chorus America and America's millions of chorus singers.* **https://www.sfcv.org/articles/feature/chorus-america-and-americas-millions-choral-singers**

99. Denney, K. (2021). *The Drive to Sing Documentary* [Film]. Kathryn Denney, Producer; Brian Denney, Director. **http://www.drivewaychoir.org**

100. For more on the benefits of singing, see:

Lee, P., Stewart, D., & Clift, S. (2018). Group singing and quality of life. In B.-L. Bartleet & L. Higgins (Eds.), *The Oxford handbook of community music* (pp. 503–524). Oxford, UK: Oxford University Press.

101. Waldinger, R., & Schulz, M. (2023). *The good life: Lessons from the world's longest scientific study of happiness.* New York: Simon & Schuster.

102. For references on musical ensembles, see:

Ansdell, G., & DeNora, T. (2016). *Musical pathways in recovery: Community music therapy and mental wellbeing.* London, UK: Routledge.

McDonald, R., Kreutz, G., & Mitchell, L. (Eds.). (2013). *Music, health, and wellbeing.* Oxford, UK: Oxford University Press.

Timmers, R., Bailes, F., & Daffern, H. (2022). *Together in music: Coordination, expression, participation.* Oxford, UK: Oxford University Press.

103. Zaki, J. (2020). *The war for kindness: Building empathy in a fractured world.* New York: Broadway Books/Penguin Random House.

104. Nields, N. & Nields, K. (2011). *All together singing in the kitchen: Creative ways to make and listen to music as a family.* Boston: Roost Books.

105. Zanes, D. (2018). *Dan Zane's house party: A family roots music treasury.* Minneapolis, MN: Quarto Publishing Group.

CHAPTER 9

106. This story excerpts an article published as:

> Hanser, S. B. (2009). In the music. *Fusion: A Magazine of Literature, Music, Art, and Ideas, 1,* 43–45.

107. Krugman, P. (2023, July 21). The Swifties are right. Concerts are worth the price. *The New York Times.*

108. Garfinkle-Crowell, S. (2023, June 17). Taylor Swift has rocked my psychiatric practice. *The New York Times.*

109. O'Neill, S. (2023, June 24). "Padam Padam": You hear it and you know it's Pride. *The New York Times.*

110. See these resources on improvisation:

> Crook, H. (2015). *How to improvise.* Winona, MN: Alfred Publishing.

> Reed, D. (2011). *Improvise for real.* David Reed, all rights reserved. **http://www.ImproviseForReal.com**

111. Csikszentmihalyi, M. (1991, 2008). *Flow: The psychology of optimal experience.* New York: Harper.

112. Keltner, D. (2023). *Awe: The new science of everyday wonder and how it can transform your life.* New York: Penguin Press.

113. Konecni, V. J. (2005). The aesthetic trinity: Awe, being moved, thrills. *Bulletin of Psychology and the Arts, 5*(2), 27–44.

114. Stellar, J. E., John-Henderson, N., Anderson, C. L., Gordon, A. M., McNeil, G. D., & Keltner, D. (2015). Positive affect and markers of inflammation: Discrete positive emotions predict lower levels of inflammatory cytokines. *Emotion, 15*(2), 129–133. **https://doi.org/10.1037/emo0000033**

115. Monroy, M., & Keltner, D. (2023). Awe as a pathway to mental and physical health. *Perspectives on Psychological Science, 18*(2), 309–320.

116. See these books by David Rothenberg:

Rothenberg, D. (2006). *Why birds sing: A journey into the mystery of bird song.* New York: Basic Books.

Rothenberg, D. (2019). *Nightingales in Berlin: Searching for the perfect sound.* Chicago, IL: University of Chicago Press.

117. Krause, B. (2013). *The great animal orchestra: Finding the origins of music in the world's wild places.* Boston: Back Bay Books.

CHAPTER 10

118. Schlein, I. (2007). *Slave songs of the United States: The complete 1867 collection of slave songs.* Milwaukee, WI: Hal Leonard.

119. Kuhn, T. S. (1962). *The structure of scientific revolutions.* Chicago, IL: University of Chicago Press.

120. See these references by Dean Keith Simonton:

Simonton, D. K. (2000). Creativity: Cognitive, personal, developmental, and social aspects. *American Psychologist, 55*(1), 151–158. **https://doi.org/10.1037/0003-066X.55.1.151**

Simonton, D. K. (1999). Creativity from a historiometric perspective. In R. J. Sternberg (Ed.), *Handbook of creativity* (pp. 116–133). Cambridge University Press.

121. Bernstein, L. (1963). *An artist's reply to violence.* Leonard Bernstein Office. **https://leonardbernstein.com/about/humanitarian/an-artists-response-to-violence**

INDEX

ABOUT THE AUTHOR

Photo by Heratch Ekmekjian

Suzanne B. Hanser is founding chair emerita and professor of music therapy at Berklee College of Music, and president of the International Association for Music & Medicine. Dr. Hanser is Past President of the World Federation of Music Therapy and National Association for Music Therapy. Other books include: *The New Music Therapist's Handbook, Integrative Health through Music Therapy: Accompanying the Journey from Illness to Wellness*, and *Manage Your Stress and Pain through Music* (book/audio), with Dr. Susan Mandel. She has published research in multidisciplinary journals, and received several awards, including the American Music Therapy Association's Lifetime Achievement Award. Her courses on music and wellness may be found on Coursera and Berklee Online.

More Fine Publications

Berklee Press

GUITAR

BERKLEE ESSENTIAL GUITAR SONGBOOK
Sheryl Bailey and Kim Perlak
00350814 Book............................ $22.99

BERKLEE GUITAR CHORD DICTIONARY
Rick Peckham
50449546 Jazz – Book $16.99
50449596 Rock – Book................. $12.99

BERKLEE GUITAR STYLE STUDIES
Jim Kelly
00200377 Book/Online Media........... $24.99

BERKLEE GUITAR THEORY
Kim Perlak
00276326 Book............................ $26.99

BLUES GUITAR TECHNIQUE
Michael Williams
50449623 Book/Online Audio $29.99

CLASSICAL TECHNIQUE FOR THE MODERN GUITARIST
Kim Perlak
00148781 Book/Online Audio.............. $19.99

COUNTRY GUITAR STYLES
Mike Ihde
00254157 Book/Online Audio............. $24.99

CREATIVE CHORDAL HARMONY FOR GUITAR
Mick Goodrick and Tim Miller
50449613 Book/Online Audio............. $24.99

FUNK/R&B GUITAR
Thaddeus Hogarth
50449569 Book/Online Audio $25.99

GUITAR SWEEP PICKING
Joe Stump
00151223 Book/Online Audio.............. $24.99

JAZZ GUITAR FRETBOARD NAVIGATION
Mark White
00154107 Book/Online Audio............. $24.99

JAZZ GUITAR IMPROVISATION STRATEGIES
Steven Kirby
00274977 Book/Online Audio............$27.99

MODAL VOICINGS FOR GUITAR
Rick Peckham
00151227 Book/Online Media $24.99

A MODERN METHOD FOR GUITAR*
William Leavitt
Volume 1: Beginner
00137387 Book/Online Video.............$27.99
Other volumes, media options, and supporting songbooks available.

A MODERN METHOD FOR GUITAR SCALES
Larry Baione
00199318 Book............................ $15.99

TRIADS FOR THE IMPROVISING GUITARIST
Jane Miller
00284857 Book/Online Audio $22.99

BASS

BASS LINES
Metal
David Marvuglio
00122465 Book/Online Audio $19.99

BERKLEE JAZZ BASS
Rich Appleman, Whit Browne, and Bruce Gertz
50449636 Book/Online Audio........... $25.99

FUNK BASS FILLS
Anthony Vitti
50449608 Book/Online Audio............$24.99

INSTANT BASS
Danny Morris
50449502 Book/CD $9.99

READING CONTEMPORARY ELECTRIC BASS
Rich Appleman
50449770 Book............................$24.99

VOICE

BELTING
Jeannie Gagné
00124984 Book/Online Media $24.99

THE CONTEMPORARY SINGER
Anne Peckham
50449595 Book/Online Audio $29.99

JAZZ VOCAL IMPROVISATION
Mili Bermejo
00159290 Book/Online Audio $19.99

TIPS FOR SINGERS
Carolyn Wilkins
50449557 Book/CD.......................... $19.95

VOCAL WORKOUTS FOR THE CONTEMPORARY SINGER
Anne Peckham
50448044 Book/Online Audio...........$27.99

YOUR SINGING VOICE
Jeannie Gagné
50449619 Book/Online Audio $34.99

WOODWINDS/BRASS

TRUMPET SOUND EFFECTS
Craig Pederson and Ueli Dörig
00121626 Book/Online Audio.................$14.99

TECHNIQUE OF THE SAXOPHONE
Joseph Viola
50449820 Volume 1.....................$24.99
50449830 Volume 2.....................$27.99
50449840 Volume 3.....................$26.99

PIANO/KEYBOARD

BERKLEE JAZZ KEYBOARD HARMONY
Suzanna Sifter
00138874 Book/Online Audio $29.99

BERKLEE JAZZ PIANO
Ray Santisi
50448047 Book/Online Audio $24.99

BERKLEE JAZZ STANDARDS FOR SOLO PIANO
Robert Christopherson, Hey Rim Jeon, Ross Ramsay, Tim Ray
00160482 Book/Online Audio.............$24.99

CHORD-SCALE IMPROVISATION FOR KEYBOARD
Ross Ramsay
50449597 Book/CD.....................$19.99

CONTEMPORARY PIANO TECHNIQUE
Stephany Tiernan
50449545 Book/Online Video $39.99

HAMMOND ORGAN COMPLETE
Dave Limina
00237801 Book/Online Audio.............$27.99

JAZZ PIANO COMPING
Suzanne Davis
50449614 Book/Online Audio $26.99

LATIN JAZZ PIANO IMPROVISATION
Rebecca Cline
50449649 Book/Online Audio............$29.99

SOLO JAZZ PIANO
Neil Olmstead
50449641 Book/Online Audio............$42.99

DRUMS/PERCUSSION

BEGINNING DJEMBE
Michael Markus and Joe Galeota
00148210 Book/Online Video...............$16.99

BERKLEE JAZZ DRUMS
Casey Scheuerell
50449612 Book/Online Audio.............$27.99

DRUM SET WARM-UPS
Rod Morgenstein
50449465 Book.........................$19.99

DRUM STUDIES
Dave Vose
50449617 Book.........................$12.99

A MANUAL FOR THE MODERN DRUMMER
Alan Dawson and Don DeMichael
50449560 Book.........................$14.99

MASTERING THE ART OF BRUSHES
Jon Hazilla
50449459 Book/Online Audio............$19.99

PHRASING: ADVANCED RUDIMENTS FOR CREATIVE DRUMMING
Russ Gold
00120209 Book/Online Media $19.99

WORLD JAZZ DRUMMING
Mark Walker
50449568 Book/CD $27.99

Berklee Press publications feature material developed at the Berklee College of Music.
To browse the complete Berklee Press Catalog, go to **www.berkleepress.com**

SONGBOOKS

NEW STANDARDS: 101 LEAD SHEETS BY WOMEN COMPOSERS MUSICIANS
Terri Lyne Carrington
00369515 Book.................................$29.99

STRINGS/ROOTS MUSIC

BERKLEE HARP
Chords, Styles, and Improvisation for Pedal and Lever Harp
Felice Pomeranz
00144263 Book/Online Audio............$26.99

BEYOND BLUEGRASS
Beyond Bluegrass Banjo
Dave Hollander and Matt Glaser
50449610 Book/CD $19.99

Beyond Bluegrass Mandolin
John McGann and Matt Glaser
50449609 Book/CD $19.99

Bluegrass Fiddle and Beyond
Matt Glaser
50449602 Book/CD $19.99

CONTEMPORARY CELLO ETUDES
Mike Block
00159292 Book/Online Audio............$24.99

EXPLORING CLASSICAL MANDOLIN
August Watters
00125040 Book/Online Media...........$24.99

FIDDLE TUNES ON JAZZ CHANGES
Matt Glaser
00120210 Book/Online Audio............$16.99

THE IRISH CELLO BOOK
Liz Davis Maxfield
50449652 Book/Online Audio $29.99

JAZZ UKULELE
Abe Lagrimas, Jr.
00121624 Book/Online Audio $26.99

BERKLEE PRACTICE METHOD

GET YOUR BAND TOGETHER
With additional volumes for other instruments, plus a teacher's guide.
Drum Set
Ron Savage, Casey Scheuerell, and the Berklee Faculty
50449429 Book/CD $19.99

Guitar
Larry Baione and the Berklee Faculty
50449426 Book/CD $29.99

Keyboard
Russell Hoffmann, Paul Schmeling, and the Berklee Faculty
50449428 Book/Online Audio $22.99

MUSIC BUSINESS

CROWDFUNDING FOR MUSICIANS
Laser Malena-Webber
00285092 Book..............................$17.99

HOW TO GET A JOB IN THE MUSIC INDUSTRY
Keith Hatschek with Breanne Beseda
00130699 Book..............................$39.99

MAKING MUSIC MAKE MONEY
Eric Beall
00355740 Book..............................$29.99

MUSIC LAW IN THE DIGITAL AGE
Allen Bargfrede
00366048 Book..............................$29.99

PROJECT MANAGEMENT FOR MUSICIANS
Jonathan Feist
50449659 Book..............................$39.99

MUSIC THEORY/EAR TRAINING

BEGINNING EAR TRAINING
Gilson Schachnik
50449548 Book/Online Audio $22.99

THE BERKLEE BOOK OF JAZZ HARMONY
Joe Mulholland and Tom Hojnacki
00113755 Book/Online Audio.............$34.99

BERKLEE CORRESPONDENCE COURSE
00244533 Book/Online Media...........$29.99

BERKLEE EAR TRAINING DUETS AND TRIOS
Gaye Tolan Hatfield
00284897 Book/Online Audio............$19.99

BERKLEE MUSIC THEORY
Paul Schmeling
50449615 **Rhythm, Scales Intervals** $29.99
50449616 **Harmony**......................$26.99

CONDUCTING MUSIC TODAY
Bruce Hangen
00237719 Book/Online Video.............$24.99

JAZZ DUETS
Richard Lowell
00302151 C Instruments.......................$14.99

MUSIC NOTATION
Mark McGrain
50449399 Theory and Technique....$29.99

REHARMONIZATION TECHNIQUES
Randy Felts
50449496 Book................................$29.99

MUSIC PRODUCTION & ENGINEERING

AUDIO MASTERING
Jonathan Wyner
50449581 Book/CD...........................$34.99

AUDIO POST PRODUCTION
Mark Cross
50449627 Book................................$32.99

CREATING COMMERCIAL MUSIC
Peter Bell
00278535 Book/Online Media $19.99

HIP-HOP PRODUCTION
Prince Charles Alexander
50449582 Book/Online Audio $24.99

THE SINGER-SONGWRITER'S GUIDE TO RECORDING IN THE HOME STUDIO
Shane Adams
00148211 Book/Online Audio..............$24.99

UNDERSTANDING AUDIO
Daniel M. Thompson
00148197 Book.................................. $49.99

WELLNESS/AUTOBIOGRAPHY

LEARNING TO LISTEN: THE JAZZ JOURNEY OF GARY BURTON
00117798 Book.................................$34.99

MANAGE YOUR STRESS AND PAIN THROUGH MUSIC
Dr. Suzanne B. Hanser and Dr. Susan E. Mandel
00117798 Book.................................$34.99

MUSICIAN'S YOGA
Mia Olson
50449587 Book.................................$26.99

THE NEW MUSIC THERAPIST'S HANDBOOK
Suzanne B. Hanser
00279325 Book.................................$34.99

SONGWRITING/COMPOSING

ARRANGING FOR HORNS
Jerry Gates
00121625 Book/Online Audio.............$24.99

ARRANGING FOR STRINGS
Mimi Rabson
00190207 Book/Online Audio.............$22.99

BEGINNING SONGWRITING
Andrea Stolpe with Jan Stolpe
00138503 Book/Online Audio $22.99

BERKLEE CONTEMPORARY MUSIC NOTATION
Jonathan Feist
00202547 Book................................ $27.99

COMPLETE GUIDE TO FILM SCORING
Richard Davis
50449607 ....$39.99

CONTEMPORARY COUNTERPOINT
Beth Denisch
00147050 Book/Online Audio............$24.99

COUNTERPOINT IN JAZZ ARRANGING
Bob Pilkington
00294301 Book/Online Audio............$29.99

THE CRAFT OF SONGWRITING
Scarlet Keys
00159283 Book/Online Audio.............$24.99

CREATIVE STRATEGIES IN FILM SCORING
Ben Newhouse
00242911 Book/Online Media.............$27.99

ESSENTIAL SONGWRITING
Jonathan Feist and Jimmy Kachulis
50448051 .... $14.99

JAZZ COMPOSITION
Ted Pease
50448000 Book/Online Audio $49.99

MELODY IN SONGWRITING
Jack Perricone
50449419 Book................................$26.99

MODERN JAZZ VOICINGS
Ted Pease and Ken Pullig
50449485 Book/Online Audio............$29.99

MUSIC COMPOSITION FOR FILM AND TELEVISION
Lalo Schifrin
50449604 Book................................$39.99

MUSIC NOTATION
50449540 **Preparing Scores & Parts**.....$25.99
50449399 **Theory and Technique**...........$29.99

POPULAR LYRIC WRITING
Andrea Stolpe
50449553 Book................................$17.99

SONGWRITING: ESSENTIAL GUIDE
Pat Pattison
50481582 **Lyric and Form Structure**.........$19.99
00124366 **Rhyming** $24.99

SONGWRITING IN PRACTICE
Mark Simos
00244545 Book................................$16.99

SONGWRITING STRATEGIES
Mark Simos
50449621 Book................................$27.99

THE SONGWRITER'S WORKSHOP
Jimmy Kachulis
50449519 **Harmony** $34.99
50449518 **Melody** $27.99

Prices subject to change without notice. Visit your local music dealer or bookstore, or go to **halleonard.com** to order

HAL•LEONARD®